Resilient Organisations

Create a Resilient Project Management and Delivery Culture

Copyright © Jeremy P Farrell 2023

All rights reserved. No part of this publication may be reproduced, stored in a retrieval system, or transmitted in any form or by any means without the prior written permission of the publisher, nor be otherwise circulated in any form of binding or cover other than that in which it is published and without a similar condition being imposed on the subsequent purchaser.

The right of Jeremy P Farrell to be identified as the author of this work has been asserted by him following the Copyright, Designs and Patents Act 1988.

V0.8

Other books in the series:

The 4 Steps of Powerful Coaching

Strengths in the Workplace

www.thegrowthlab.org

authors@thegrowthlab.org

jp@jpfarrell.co.uk

Contents

Foreword 11
Introduction 13
Project Delivery 17
    Your Project Delivery Playbook 19
    Playbook contents 20
    Activity: An early wireframe 22
Organisational culture and climate 25
    Culture 25
    Climate 25
Contributing factors to organisational culture 28
    Summarising determinants of culture 32
    Indicators of a positive organisational culture 36
    Summarising factors of a positive organisational culture 37
    Positive leadership competencies 38
    Healthy project delivery environments 42
    Summarising a healthy delivery culture 43
    Toxic delivery environments and culture 45
Resilience 47
    Resilient people 51
    Summarising personal resilience 53
    Resilient Organisations 55
    What is a Resilient organisation? 57
    Summarising resilient organisational factors 60

- Positive Leadership in Project Delivery 61
  - Agile Organisations 65
  - Organisational Agility 66
  - Summarising agile organisations 68
- The importance of understanding teams 73
  - The difference between project teams and regular teams ... 74
  - Psychological safety in delivery teams 78
  - Creating psychologically safe project teams 82
- Project Managers' fears 84
  - What are project managers' career fears? 85
  - What causes project managers to resign? 89
  - Creating a healthy project and team climate 92
- Project health 95
  - Key project health measures 96
  - Summarising key project health measures 98
  - Troubled projects 99
  - What are the signs of a troubled project? 100
  - Summarising troubled project indicators 101
  - Key project board leadership levers 103
- Implementing change with the E4 Xchange Leadership Model 109
  - Employee Engagement Opportunities™ 111
  - The model starts with Engagement 112
  - A people-centric approach 114
  - It is action-oriented. 115
  - It is performance-driven. 115

It is agile..115
E4XLM – Implementing your change.............................117
    Engage 117
    Engaging with openness and honesty 119
    Enable..124
    Encourage and Empower 126
    Evaluate...134
    Transformational Leadership 139
Building your playbook...143
    What should be in a project delivery vision statement?.....143
    What should be in a project team mission statement? 148
Examples of project delivery vision statements:.....................150
    A software development department:................150
    A hospital project delivery team: 150
    A civil engineering company...............................150
    Your Vision: 152
    Guiding Principles for your project delivery culture while building this Playbook: 155
High-performing teams 158
    What good looks like for our teams, and what we will do to achieve and sustain it 160
Poor project delivery 163
    What poor delivery looks like for us, and what will we do to improve it 164
Key health indicators 167
    1. Key Project Health Indicators in Engineering: 167
    2. Key Project Health Indicators in Software Engineering:..167

- 3. Key Project Health Indicators in Healthcare: 168
- Key health indicators that will guide us 170

Managing by Exception 173
- 1. Engineering: 173
- 2. Software Engineering: 173
- 3. Healthcare: 173
- Exception approach 176

Project Management methodologies in industries 179
- 1. Engineering: 179
- 2. Software Engineering: 179
- 3. Healthcare: 179
- Project Delivery Methodology: 182

Project Management tools 185
- 1. Engineering: 185
- 2. Software Engineering: 185
- 3. Healthcare: 185
- Project Management Tools: 188

Project Management Roles and Responsibilities 191
- 1. Project Board: 191
- 2. Project Manager: 192
- 3. Team Manager: 192
- Roles and Responsibilities: 194

Project Team Management Principles 197
- Team management 198

Risk Management examples 201
- 1. Engineering Projects: 201

- 2. Software Engineering Projects: 201
  - Risk Management: 204
- Change Management failures 207
  - 1. Engineering Projects: 207
  - 2. Software Engineering Projects: 207
  - 3. Healthcare Projects: 208
  - Change Management: 210
- Project Quality Assurance 213
  - 1. Engineering Projects: 213
  - 2. Software Engineering Projects: 213
  - 3. Healthcare Projects: 214
  - Quality Assurance: 216
- Project Delivery Assurance 219
  - Project Assurance: 222
- Stakeholder Communication 225
  - 1. Engineering Projects: 225
  - 2. Software Engineering Projects: 225
  - 3. Healthcare Projects: 226
  - Communication Plan: 228
- Good Project Closeout 231
  - 1. Engineering Projects: 231
  - 2. Software Engineering Projects: 231
  - 3. Healthcare Projects: 232
  - Project Closeout: 234
- Lessons Learned 237
  - 1. Engineering Projects: 237

2. Software Engineering Projects: 237

 3. Healthcare Projects: 238

 Lessons Learned: 239

 Glossary: 242

Appendices 243

 Key service delivery measures 243

 What should be in a service delivery vision statement? 245

 Sources of research into project failure? 247

 Which industry has the greatest project manager attrition?
 249

 What is the research into project failure? 250

 What are the main findings of the Standish Group CHAOS Report? 252

 Key Research into Toxic Cultures 254

Foreword

The output of working through this book and doing the summary exercises at the end is a playbook for creating or building on, or recovering, a resilient project delivery culture.

A playbook is a document that outlines a set of standardised procedures, policies, or guidelines for a particular activity or process. The term is commonly used in business, sports, and military contexts.

A playbook typically includes detailed instructions, checklists, and guidelines for specific situations or scenarios that may arise during the activity or process. Individuals or teams involved in the activity can use it as a reference guide to ensure consistency, reduce errors, and improve performance.

In a business context, a playbook may refer to a set of documented procedures, policies, or best practices for a specific business function, such as sales, marketing, or customer service. The playbook may guide employees, standardise procedures across different departments or teams, and ensure the organisation's goals are met.

In sports, a playbook typically refers to a collection of offensive and defensive plays a team uses during a game. The playbook is developed by coaches and tailored to the team's strengths, weaknesses, and opponents.

A playbook may refer to procedures, tactics, and strategies for various combat scenarios in military contexts. Playbooks may be developed for individual soldiers, teams, or units to ensure they are prepared for different situations and can respond quickly and effectively.

This book is both information and a workbook as we explore your project and service delivery culture. This is not a book about project management tools and techniques but rather about leadership and management of a project or service delivery organisation. We seek to walk step by step, creating a picture of a healthy project delivery culture within which project managers are empowered to take responsibility and take appropriate risks without fear of retribution. This is not a get-out-of-jail card for a project manager taking ill-considered risks that could affect the project, organisation, function, or reputation but rather taking informed risks based on experience and seeking appropriate advice from subject matter experts.

Although we see a playbook as starting with your vision and principles for a healthy project and service delivery culture, we will only address those two parts at the end of this book as you have worked your way through what good looks like for your organisation and what essential management systems and accountability structures you will put in place. We may start with an essential vision for your department. Ultimately, we will refine this with a vision and principles for a sustained improvement in culture and climate, leading to resilient project managers and consistent project delivery.

In the following sections, we will look at what we mean by project delivery and organisational culture and what we mean by a project delivery culture and a healthy project management and service delivery culture.

Introduction

The book has been written to enable you as a manager to take the best of shared wisdom and proven actions and compile a playbook from which you can create and implement initiatives to create and reinforce your high-performance project management culture.

Knowing that around 50% of projects still fail to produce the appropriate business benefits, we can confidently say that many organisations struggle to create or sustain high-performance delivery cultures. High-performance delivery is not only about achieving business benefits on the top or bottom lines. Performance is also what attracts and retains project management talent in your organisation. There is a global shortage of experienced and capable project managers, and many companies are promoting themselves as the employer of choice for them. Retention of project managers is critical to your success as you retain their institutional memory and network of colleagues, which cannot be replaced by a new hire, no matter how good they are.

Each of us seeks to find meaningful work which more than fills most of our days, and some of the most rewarding work we have had is on projects. Projects often create change; therefore, as team members, we contribute to change within our environment. Participating in the change process can make our work more meaningful than being in a process-driven operational environment. This statement is not to say there is anything unmeaningful in process and operations. To be a resilient and engaging project delivery environment, we must have a stable foundation of processes, procedures, methods, and tools.

There are two primary ways you can work through this book. One way is to work through the book sequentially, attempting to build from the more general to the specific. Firstly, we look at organisational culture as the playbook's primary objective is creating a culture. Next, we look at project delivery and what makes a healthy and resilient organisation and stuff. We look at what we can do to encourage and enable changes in behaviours and attitudes, flowing into changes in culture and, hopefully, climate. We then use the book's final third to look at what you want to achieve under each heading within the playbook. In the paperback version, we have left some space on each page to make notes about the actions you want to prioritise for the section and, therefore, as the outcome of working through this material.

The other way you can work through the book is as a reference guide you can dip into when you want to remind yourself of these dimensions of a delivery environment and delivery culture and find some inspiration for actions you can initiate to improve your situation.

Regardless of the approach you take to the book, the prompts in Part 3 cannot be more prescriptive or facilitate the brainstorming you would need to do on your own and with colleagues to drive out the options you have to implement some of the actions listed in part two of the book. The prompts take the familiar format of defining the goal you want to achieve under that heading, then, considering the current situation, brainstorm options you might have in the short, near, or medium term. Having created a list of realistic options, you can choose some and be more specific in defining those you will implement soonest. You should apply the heuristic of ensuring the goals are specific, measurable, aligned with your strategy, realistic, and time-boxed.

We must embrace the slight irony that we need a project to adapt or adopt new approaches to project delivery, but there it is! This project is an opportunity to consciously apply some of the theory as you start to practise what you preach and implement change that people will follow.

The book provides a great deal of information in bullet form, making it concise and easy to read. We do not spend pages explaining each of the elements of the book, believing that often less is more and your time is precious. Each of these suggested actions that can be taken can be unpacked at length, and maybe the subject of another book aims to be more descriptive for those who would study further. The book is designed to be scribbled on and marked up. Whether reading it on an e-reader where you can highlight and make notes, having the paperback in your hands, or printing out specific pages, you are encouraged to interact with the material rather than scan over the topics and actions. True learning and practical implementation result from interaction with the content and discussion with your colleagues.

You might use different colours to indicate those actions you want to prioritise or number them in order of priority to you, choose the quickest wins, or use the MoSCoW acronym. For example, you could mark every action in a section as those you must do, should do, could do or will not do. This makes for a rapid reference when reviewing the book and deciding what to work on next. This MoSCoW prioritisation fits nicely with an agile approach to implementing your changes incrementally and iteratively, working with a cross-functional team of subject matter experts, business analysts, and organisational change specialists. Because your changes are to how you work and will be implemented incrementally, you can give that team a significant amount of leeway to make their own decisions without damaging operations or the organisation.

Suppose you choose a more traditional waterfall approach to the project instead of Agile. In that case, you could end up applying more significant changes at a single time than your staff could feel comfortable with, undermining the very objective of the project in the first place.

Your approach should be tailored to your organisation's requirements and the level of change at which you are aiming.

Project Delivery

Project delivery refers to completing and delivering a project to its stakeholders, on time, within budget, and according to its scope and quality requirements. It involves coordinating and managing various tasks, resources, and activities to achieve project objectives and meet stakeholder expectations.

The project delivery process typically includes several stages: planning, execution, monitoring, and closure. The project objectives, scope, timelines, budget, and resources are defined during the planning stage, and the project plan is created. The execution stage involves implementing the project plan, monitoring progress, and adjusting plans as needed. The monitoring stage involves tracking progress, identifying and addressing issues, and reporting to stakeholders. Finally, the closure stage involves completing and delivering the project to the stakeholders, often including the post-project evaluation and lessons learned.

Project delivery success depends on many factors, such as effective communication, strong leadership, efficient use of resources, risk management, and stakeholder management. A well-managed project delivery process can lead to improved project outcomes, increased stakeholder satisfaction, and a positive impact on the organisation's bottom line.

The output of this book, and the associated course, is a playbook of how you will approach creating or improving your project management and delivery culture. In some places, you will see references to an associated course which we deliver online, part-time, over seven days. Still, we suggest you can replace that course if you work with some qualified organisational development consultants inside or outside of your organisation.

The course we deliver is live and online with a restricted number of participants. We provide a cohort-based experience of people from multiple organisations. As a result, you will benefit from various perspectives from different industries and technical environments.

Your Project Delivery Playbook

A project delivery playbook is a comprehensive document that outlines the best practices, procedures, and guidelines for delivering successful projects within an organisation.

The Resilient Project Management and Delivery Culture playbook you will create in this book may include the following:

- Your Vision
- Guiding Principles
- What good looks like
- What poor delivery looks like
- Key health indicators
- Exception approach
- Project Delivery Methodology
- Roles and Responsibilities
- Communication Plan
- Risk Management
- Project Management Tools
- Change Management
- Quality Assurance
- Lessons Learned
- Project Closeout
- Glossary

Playbook contents

The contents of a project delivery playbook may vary depending on the organisation's size, industry, and project management approach. However, some essential components of a project delivery playbook may include the following:

Project Delivery Methodology: The playbook should outline the organisation's preferred project delivery methodology, including a step-by-step process for executing projects.

Roles and Responsibilities: The playbook should describe the roles and responsibilities of project team members, stakeholders, and other contributors involved in project delivery.

Communication Plan: The playbook should include a communication plan that outlines how stakeholders will be informed and engaged throughout the project lifecycle.

Risk Management: The playbook should identify potential risks and describe the organisation's approach to managing and mitigating them.

Project Management Tools: The playbook should list the project management tools and software used to manage the project.

Change Management: The playbook should outline how project scope, timeline, or budget changes will be managed and communicated.

Quality Assurance: The playbook should include quality assurance procedures and standards that will be followed to ensure project deliverables meet the required standards.

Lessons Learned: The playbook should detail how project outcomes will be evaluated and how the organisation will learn from past experiences to improve future projects.

Project Closeout: The playbook should describe the project closeout process, including the final review, sign-off, and handover to stakeholders.

Glossary: The playbook should include a glossary of key terms and definitions to ensure a common understanding of project management language within the organisation.

Overall, the project delivery playbook should serve as a reference guide for all project team members, providing a common approach to project delivery that ensures successful outcomes.

The Resilient Project Management and Service Delivery Culture playbook you will create in this book will include the following:

Your Vision: A vision for project delivery

Guiding Principles: A set of guiding principles for all staff in project and service delivery

What good looks like

What poor delivery looks like

Key health indicators

Exception approach

Activity: An early wireframe

Mark one or many of the following aspects that you DO NOT want to have in your Playbook to Build a Resilient Project and Delivery Culture:

- Vision for the Project Delivery Culture
- Guiding principles of your project and service delivery teams
- What a good project delivery culture looks like
- What a poor project delivery culture looks like
- Project Health indicator definitions
- Project Delivery Methodology
- Roles and Responsibilities
- Communication Plan
- Risk Management
- Project Management Tools
- Change Management
- Quality Assurance
- Project Assurance
- Lessons Learned
- Project Closeout
- Service Delivery Methodology
- Service Level Agreements (SLAs)
- Service Management Tools
- Service Improvement Plan
- Service Delivery Closeout
- Glossary

Overall, the project delivery playbook should serve as a reference guide for all project team members, providing a common approach to project delivery that ensures successful outcomes.

Let us now explore organisational culture as a context for the playbook.

Part 1
Exploring organisational culture and resilience

Organisational culture and climate

Organisational culture and organisational climate are related concepts that describe different aspects of an organisation's working environment.

Culture

Organisational culture refers to the shared values, beliefs, assumptions, and behaviours characterising an organisation. It represents the underlying beliefs, values, and attitudes that shape how people think and behave in the organisation. Organisational culture is often described as the "personality" of an organisation. It can be thought of as the organisation's collective identity.

Organisational culture refers to the specific aspects of the work environment that affect employees' perceptions of the organisation. It is the "**atmosphere**" of the organisation that employees experience in their daily work. Organisational culture includes communication patterns, leadership style, job demands, rewards and recognition, and the physical environment.

Culture can be considered as '**How we do things around here**.'

Climate

On the other hand, organisational **climate** is often described as the "**mood**" of an organisation. So the climate is '**How we feel about how we do things around here**.'

While there is some overlap between organisational culture and organisational climate, they are different concepts. Organisational **culture is more deeply ingrained and enduring**, while **organisational climate is more situational and subject to change**. In addition, organisational culture tends to be relatively stable over time. In contrast, external factors and organisational changes can influence organisational climate.

In summary, culture and climate are essential in understanding an organisation's working environment. They can significantly impact employee behaviour, attitudes, and performance.

"The only thing of real importance that leaders do is to create and manage culture."

Edgar Schein

Attributes of organisational culture:

Leadership

Team dynamics

Communication

Values and beliefs

Norms and practices

Traditions and rituals

Diversity and inclusion

Attitudes and emotions

Contributing factors to organisational culture

Organisational culture is built on shared values and beliefs that guide the behaviour of team members. Communication is a critical aspect of organisational culture, with effective communication helping to build trust, alignment, and engagement. Leaders play a crucial role in shaping the culture. Their behaviour and communication set the tone for the rest of the organisation's interactions – how it handles conflict, direction, and consultation.

An organisation's culture is also shaped by the norms and practices defining work, such as decision-making processes, feedback mechanisms, and performance evaluation systems. The dynamics between team members also contribute to the culture, with positive and supportive relationships helping to build a healthy work environment. The attitudes and emotions of team members are significant, with positive attitudes and emotions helping to build a culture of collaboration, innovation, and creativity.

Traditions and rituals, such as team-building exercises, recognition programs, and company events, can also shape organisational culture – literally 'the way we do things around here'. The degree to which an organisation values and promotes diversity and inclusion can also be an essential aspect of organisational culture.

The nature and strength of organisational culture are well illustrated when one looks at the overall behaviours of some organisations in the public eye. For example, where corruption becomes endemic in a parastatal organisation, an attitude of entitlement, nepotism, and theft of physical or financial resources becomes a norm.

Alternatively, one might think about some security services where it would appear that there is a culture of racism or misogyny or think about something more commercial where fraud is occurring in manipulating results related to environmental emissions. These are examples of negative cultural forces within the organisation.

Positive examples are not difficult to find if you are looking for them, or if you are part of an organisation with a compassionate culture, solid values and a mission or vision of which you can be proud. For example, some of the world's largest and most demanding commercial organisations have strong brands in the marketplace. Still, they have also created strong employer and employee brand identities.

One good example is IBM, which has exceptionally high-performance expectations. Because of that, employees are proud to say I am an IBMer.

As a proud ex-IBMer (I'm not sure you ever become an actual 'ex' because of the relationships formed in the fire!), let me expand on their culture here.

If you do not know about IBM, IBM (International Business Machines Corporation) is a technology company that has been in operation for over a century. The company was founded in 1911 and has grown to become one of the most successful technology companies in the world. Here are some factors that have contributed to IBM's resilience over the years:

The company's robust corporate culture emphasizes innovation, teamwork, and customer satisfaction. It has a long-standing commitment to excellence and has a reputation for delivering high-quality products and services. In addition, IBM has had strong and stable leadership over the years.

The company has been led by some of history's most successful and visionary CEOs, including Thomas J. Watson Sr., Lou Gerstner, and Ginni Rometty. These leaders have guided the company through times of change and uncertainty and have been instrumental in IBM's success. For example, Lou Gerstner shook things up without disrupting the culture negatively when he came in from American Express and challenged IBM to think like the customer. His book 'Elephants can dance' tells this story.

Over the years, IBM's rich culture has enabled it to attract and retain top talent. From its early days as a maker of tabulating machines to its current position as a leader in the technology industry, IBM has always placed a premium on innovation, collaboration, and employee respect.

One of the hallmarks of IBM's culture is its **focus on innovation**. The company has a long history of developing new technologies and products that have transformed our lives and work. This focus on innovation has partly been driven by the company's commitment to research and development. Over the years, IBM has invested heavily in R&D and has a reputation for being a leader in many areas of technology, including artificial intelligence, cloud computing, and quantum computing.

Another critical aspect of IBM's culture is **collaboration**. The company has a strong tradition of working closely with customers, partners, and other stakeholders to develop solutions that meet their needs. This collaborative approach has helped IBM build strong relationships with its customers, enabling it to win new business and retain existing customers over the long term.

Respect for employees is a core value at IBM. The company is known for its inclusive and diverse workplace, where employees are encouraged to bring their whole selves to work.

IBM has also pioneered flexible work arrangements, allowing employees to work remotely and on flexible schedules. These policies have helped IBM attract and retain top talent, particularly in software development and data science.

In addition to these core values, IBM has been known for its **strong leadership** and **corporate governance**. The company has a long history of **ethical business practices**. In addition, it has been recognized for its **commitment to sustainability and social responsibility**. These values have helped IBM to build a reputation as **a trustworthy and reliable partner** for its customers and stakeholders.

Overall, IBM's culture has played a critical role in enabling the company to attract and retain top talent. By emphasizing innovation, collaboration, and employee respect, IBM has created a challenging and rewarding workplace. Of course, IBM's culture will continue to evolve as the technology industry continues. Still, its **commitment to its core values will likely remain constant**.

Other global brands that foster a similar brand identity that employees can be proud of include Microsoft and Google. Granted, these technology companies can invest in innovation significantly and rapidly. However, other corporations that have survived the changes and turbulence of time are:

Amazon: Amazon is often cited as one of the most resilient companies in the world, thanks to its ability to innovate and adapt quickly to changing market conditions.

Toyota: Toyota has long been regarded as one of the most resilient companies in the automotive industry, thanks to its focus on quality, efficiency, and continuous improvement.

Johnson & Johnson: Johnson & Johnson is often cited as a model of corporate resilience, thanks to its ability to weather multiple crises over the years, including product recalls and lawsuits.

The Red Cross: The Red Cross is known for its resilience in natural disasters, war, and other humanitarian crises, thanks to its global network of volunteers and donors.

The United Nations: The UN has demonstrated remarkable resilience over the years, weathering multiple crises and adapting to changing global conditions.

The World Health Organization (WHO): The WHO is often cited as a model of resilience in the face of global health emergencies, thanks to its ability to coordinate international response efforts and mobilize resources. None is more evident than the response to the COVID-19 pandemic.

Procter & Gamble: Procter & Gamble is known for its resilience in changing consumer preferences and market conditions, thanks to its focus on innovation and brand management.

I am sure you can think of many other companies contributing to society and the world's well-being as manufacturers, farmers, transportation, and often in disaster relief organisations or global associations.

Summarising determinants of culture

Values and beliefs: Organisational culture is built on shared values and beliefs that guide the behaviour of team members.

Communication: Communication is a critical aspect of organisational culture, with effective communication helping to build trust, alignment, and engagement.

Leadership: Leaders play a crucial role in shaping organisational culture, with their behaviour and communication setting the tone for the rest of the organisation.

Norms and practices: Organisational culture is also shaped by the norms and practices that define how work is done, such as decision-making processes, feedback mechanisms, and performance evaluation systems.

Team dynamics: The dynamics between team members also contribute to organisational culture, with positive and supportive relationships helping to build a healthy work environment.

Attitudes and emotions: The attitudes and emotions of team members also shape organisational culture, with positive attitudes and emotions helping to build a culture of collaboration, innovation, and creativity.

Traditions and rituals: Organisational culture can also be shaped by traditions and rituals, such as team-building exercises, recognition programs, and company events.

Diversity and inclusion: The degree to which an organisation values and promotes diversity and inclusion can also be an essential aspect of organisational culture.

Overall, organisational culture is a complex and multifaceted concept shaped by various factors that define the work environment and its values and beliefs.

Of course, we are most interested in what makes a healthy and resilient organisational culture versus an unhealthy or toxic work environment. So which of the above factors do you think to carry the most weight within your organisational culture?

Let us look at what constitutes a positive or healthy organisational culture and what is evidence of a good workplace.

"Culture is a reflection of leadership."

Simon Sinek

Characteristics of a positive culture:

Trust and respect

Positive leadership

Learning and growth

Open communication

Innovation and creativity

Recognition and celebration

A Strong sense of purpose and values

Collaboration and teamwork

Indicators of a positive organisational culture

A positive culture is built on a shared sense of purpose and values, which help to align and motivate team members. Effective communication is vital, with team members encouraged to share their ideas, feedback, and concerns. A supportive culture is built on trust and respect, with team members valuing each other's contributions and treating each other with fairness and empathy.

Collaboration and teamwork are encouraged, with team members working together to achieve shared goals. Positive leadership drives a positive culture, where leaders model and reinforce the values and behaviours underpinning a healthy work environment.

Drawing on the earlier example of IBM's culture, they demand that their executives follow core leadership competencies. In addition, team members are encouraged to develop their skills and knowledge, and there are opportunities for professional growth and advancement.

An innovative culture is open to new ideas and approaches, with team members encouraged to be creative and innovative.

Finally, in a positive culture, team members are recognised and celebrated for their achievements, which helps to build morale and motivation.

Summarising factors of a positive organisational culture

A Strong sense of purpose and values: A positive culture is built on a shared sense of purpose and values.

Open communication: Effective communication is critical in a resilient culture.

Trust and respect: A positive culture is built on trust and respect.

Collaboration and teamwork: Collaboration and teamwork are expected in cultures of continual improvement.

Positive leadership: Positive culture is driven by positive leadership.

Learning and growth: Team members are encouraged to develop their skills and knowledge.

Innovation and creativity: New ideas and approaches are welcomed.

Recognition and celebration: Team members are recognised and celebrated for their achievements.

Positive leadership competencies

Simon Sinek is a well-known leadership expert who believes that the best leaders prioritise their team's needs and lead by example. According to Sinek, effective leadership requires a set of competencies that go beyond technical skills and experience.

One of the critical competencies that Sinek emphasizes is the ability to build trust and create a sense of safety within a team. This involves being vulnerable and admitting mistakes, as well as actively listening to and valuing the opinions of others.

Another critical competency is inspiring and motivating others through a clear and compelling vision. Sinek emphasizes the importance of communicating a sense of purpose and direction that resonates with team members and helps them understand how their work contributes to the organisation's overall goals.

Sinek also stresses the importance of empathy and the ability to understand and connect with team members on a personal level. This includes being able to recognize and respond to their needs, as well as being willing to provide support and guidance when necessary.

Overall, Sinek's view on leadership competencies emphasizes the importance of building solid relationships with team members, creating a sense of purpose and direction, and being willing to listen, support, and guide others towards success.

In his best-selling book, "Start with Why," Sinek explores the idea that the most successful organizations and leaders start by asking "why" they do what they do rather than just focusing on "what" they do or "how" they do it.

The book argues that starting with why - understanding the purpose and beliefs that drive an organization or individual - can inspire loyalty, trust, and a sense of shared purpose among customers, employees, and other stakeholders.

Sinek uses examples of successful companies and leaders, such as Apple and Martin Luther King Jr., to illustrate how a clear understanding of why they exist and what they believe has helped them create a loyal following and achieve long-term success.

The book also emphasizes the importance of communicating the "why" clearly and compellingly through a message that resonates emotionally with others.

Overall, Sinek's book encourages individuals and organizations to focus on their purpose and values as a starting point for success rather than just their products or services.

"It's not just about skill or talent; it's about character and personality as well. You need to have a good mix of players who are not just good footballers, but also good human beings."

Jurgen Klopp

Characteristics of a healthy team culture:

Trust

Respect

Learning

Collaboration

Accountability

Clear communication

Healthy project delivery environments

Healthy delivery culture exhibits the same attributes as a healthy and positive organisational culture.

A healthy delivery culture is a working environment where project managers and team members feel valued, respected, and supported and where collaboration, communication, and trust are actively promoted. It is a culture that encourages constructive feedback and continuous learning and improvement.

Colleagues communicate effectively and efficiently, sharing information and actively listening to each other. They trust each other to deliver on commitments and to be honest and transparent in their work. Peers work together to achieve common goals, leveraging each other's strengths and skills to drive success, taking responsibility for their work and holding each other accountable for meeting shared goals. They respect each other's opinions, ideas, and contributions, regardless of their position or seniority.

The culture encourages individual and collective continuous learning, growth, and development. A healthy delivery culture promotes a positive and productive working environment, increasing motivation, job satisfaction, and, ultimately, better outcomes for the organisation.

Summarising a healthy delivery culture

Clear communication: Team members communicate effectively and efficiently.

Trust: Team members trust each other to deliver on commitments and to be honest and transparent in their work.

Collaboration: Colleagues leverage each other's strengths and skills to drive success.

Accountability: Teams take responsibility for their work and hold each other accountable for meeting shared goals.

Respect: There is respect for each other's opinions, ideas, and contributions, regardless of position or seniority.

Learning: The delivery culture encourages continuous learning, growth, and development, individually and collectively.

***

The descriptions and summaries of a healthy organisational and delivery culture are at one end of a spectrum of cultures. At the other end of the spectrum is what can be called a toxic organisational or project delivery culture, which is demonstrated by poor quality results, staff turnover, and regretted attrition. Unfortunately, when people leave voluntarily due to unhappiness and attractive offers from other employers, it is often the people that you would very much prefer to stay with your organisation.

Toxic delivery environments:

Blame culture

Lack of accountability

Resistance to change

Poor communication

Unhealthy competition

Toxic delivery environments and culture

A toxic project culture is one in which the values, norms, and behaviours of the project team and/or organisation are harmful, dysfunctional, or counterproductive. A toxic project culture can have a range of negative impacts on the project, team members, and the broader organisation, including reduced productivity, increased turnover, and damage to morale and motivation.

Instead of seeking to write paragraphs and pages on what toxic culture looks like, it is fair to say that toxic is the extreme or polar opposite of healthy and resilient delivery cultures. Therefore we will summarise some common characteristics of toxic project culture, including the following:

Blame culture: When project teams are quick to blame individuals or groups for mistakes or failures, it can create a negative and stressful work environment that erodes trust and discourages collaboration.

Lack of accountability: A toxic project culture can also be characterised by a lack of accountability. Team members avoid taking responsibility for their actions or decisions, or leaders fail to hold team members accountable for their work.

Resistance to change: Colleagues or teams that are resistant to change or unwilling to adapt to new ideas, approaches, or technologies can stifle innovation and creativity and lead to a stagnant and demotivating work environment.

Poor communication: When communication is inconsistent, unclear, or ineffective, it can lead to misunderstandings, misaligned expectations, and a lack of trust and transparency among team members.

Unhealthy competition: A delivery culture prioritising competition over collaboration can create a cutthroat work environment that discourages teamwork and undermines project success.

Addressing a toxic project culture requires a combination of individual and organisational-level interventions, including clear communication, leadership support, feedback mechanisms, and opportunities for team members to engage in open and constructive dialogue. A healthy project culture is characterised by trust, collaboration, and a shared commitment to project success.

There is a growing body of research on toxic project cultures, particularly in the field of project management. Some of the critical research in this area is listed in the Appendix.

These studies and others suggest that toxic project cultures can significantly negatively impact project outcomes and employee well-being, highlighting the importance of addressing toxic behaviours and promoting a healthy project culture.

Resilience

My experience as an engineer taught me a few things about the strengths of materials and architecture, which make for good illustrations of 'resilience'.

I trust they will provide you with an understanding of the current business concept relating to people and organisations.

Bridging the gap consistently

You may remember, or you may now take note, that when you're approaching a bridge and going over along the bridge, that repeated bumping that you either hear or feel depending on how old your car is. that sound is the result of intentional gaps in the road which allows for expansion and contraction without cracking the tarmac. You can imagine this might have been learnt the hard way but is now designed into your bridges and roads at particular junctures.

All at sea

When you look out into the ocean and see a large ship sailing by, you see something exceptionally strong and able to with stand wind and waves in extreme conditions. These ships cannot survive because of their strength alone but because of the flexibility inherent in their design, allowing them to twist or bend within acceptable tolerances. The naval architect will not design long vessels to be rigid. One reason is that it would be simply too expensive, and you would try to build smaller vessels. Still, the other is that you would be asking for structural failure.

The strength of the ship and its ability to with stand extreme conditions comes from its flexibility and ability to bounce back.

Blowing in the wind

You will have noticed the somewhat ridiculous need for countries to build skyscrapers taller than each other, the limits now down to the metre and the foot as they push to the extremes of architectural flexibility. These buildings are so tall that they have a 'sail area', which also requires some movement in high winds.

For example, the Burj Khalifa in Dubai says up to 2 metres on the 163rd floor. This is another example of where resilience is because the design allows for flex rather than standing up entirely to the wind. In addition, the core of the building and the foundation are built to carry the changing stresses without snapping.

***

Hopefully, this gives you context when we next use the word resilience in human and organisational terms.

"Resilience is not what happens to you. It's how you react to, respond to, and recover from what happens to you."

Jeffrey Gitomer

Characteristics of resilient people:

Self-care

Social support

Positive mindset

Emotional regulation

Problem-solving skills

Flexibility and adaptability

Resilient people

In today's fast-paced and ever-changing world, individuals face many challenges and adversities, from personal crises to global pandemics. Some individuals can navigate these challenges and emerge stronger. In contrast, others struggle to cope and may experience long-term adverse effects on their well-being.

Resilience is the ability to adapt and thrive in the face of adversity. Understanding what makes individuals resilient is increasingly vital for individuals, organizations, and society.

Studying resilient individuals can provide valuable insights into the strategies and practices that enable people to overcome adversity and build psychological and emotional strength. In addition, by understanding the factors contributing to resilience, individuals can better prepare for future challenges and improve their ability to recover quickly from setbacks.

Examining resilient individuals can also inform best practices for healthcare providers, educators, and policymakers, helping them develop interventions and programs that foster resilience in their communities.

Resilient people can adapt and bounce back from challenging or stressful situations in their personal and professional lives. They possess the ability to maintain a positive attitude and cope with adversity. They can learn from difficult experiences and use them as opportunities for growth and development.

Resilient people tend to have a positive outlook on life, focusing on what they can control and finding the positives in even the most challenging situations. They can manage their emotions and maintain a sense of calm and perspective, even in stressful or difficult situations. They can approach problems with a solution-focused mindset and are adept at finding creative and practical solutions to challenges.

Resilient people can adapt to changing circumstances and are flexible in approaching challenges. In addition, resilient people tend to have strong social support networks, which provide emotional support and practical assistance when needed. Resilience also comes from prioritising self-care, including regular exercise, healthy eating, and getting enough rest to maintain physical and emotional well-being.

In summary, resilient people are better equipped to cope with stress and adversity, which can help them maintain their overall well-being and succeed in their personal and professional lives.

Summarising personal resilience

Understanding what makes individuals resilient is crucial not only for individual well-being but also for the broader society. By fostering resilience, individuals can better navigate challenges and contribute to the resilience of their communities and the broader ecosystem in which they operate.

Positive mindset: Resilient people tend to have a positive outlook on life.

Emotional regulation: Resilient people can manage their emotions and maintain a sense of calm and perspective.

Problem-solving skills: Resilient people can approach problems with a solution-focused mindset, finding creative and practical solutions to challenges.

Flexibility and adaptability: Resilient people can adapt to changing circumstances and are flexible in their approach to challenges.

Social support: Resilient people tend to have strong social support networks.

Self-care: Resilient people prioritise self-care.

"You may encounter many defeats, but you must not be defeated. In fact, it may be necessary to encounter the defeats, so you can know who you are, what you can rise from, how you can still come out of it."

Maya Angelou

Characteristics of resilient organisations:

Strong leadership

Clear and flexible strategy

Agile and empowered teams

Robust and adaptable systems

Continuous learning and improvement

Strong relationships and communication

What is a Resilient organisation?

In today's fast-paced and constantly changing business environment, the ability of organizations to survive and thrive in the face of unexpected challenges and uncertainties has become increasingly important. Resilient organizations can adapt and recover quickly from disruptions, including economic downturns, natural disasters, cyber-attacks, and pandemics.

Resilience is a critical factor in an organization's long-term success. It allows companies to maintain their competitive edge and emerge stronger from challenging times. Research has shown that companies that demonstrate resilience are more likely to achieve sustainable growth and maintain profitability over the long-term.

Studying resilient organizations can provide valuable insights into the strategies and practices that enable companies to weather crises and emerge stronger. By understanding the factors contributing to resilience, organizations can better prepare for future disruptions and improve their ability to recover quickly from unexpected events.

Furthermore, examining resilient organizations can also inform best practices for leaders and managers, helping them develop the skills and competencies necessary to build a resilient culture within their organizations.

Just as it is essential for individuals, understanding why organizations are resilient is crucial for individual organizations, the broader business community, and society. By fostering resilience, organizations can better navigate uncertainty and contribute to the resilience of the broader ecosystem in which they operate.

For his landmark book "Good to Great", Jim Collins investigated how some companies could transform themselves from good to great ones, achieving exceptional success. Collins and his team studied companies that outperformed their peers by at least ten times over 15 years, examining the factors that contributed to their success.

Collins identified several key factors that separated these companies from their competitors, including the importance of having what he calls a 'Level 5' leader who embodies a combination of personal humility and professional will, developing a culture of discipline, embracing a rigorous analytical approach, focusing on the right people and their roles, and creating a culture of commitment to the company's core values.

As we have seen earlier, IBM is a classic example of these traits.

Resilient organisations adapt to changing circumstances and recover quickly from disruptions, setbacks, and unexpected events. They anticipate and respond to challenges effectively and efficiently and maintain high levels of performance and productivity in the face of adversity.

Resilient organisations have a clear vision and strategy that are flexible enough to adapt to changing circumstances. In addition, they have strong and effective leaders who can guide the organisation through challenging times and make difficult decisions.

These robust and responsive organisations have systems and processes that are robust and adaptable, allowing them to respond quickly and effectively to unexpected events.

Resilient organisations were never more visible than those which were able to batten down the hatches and be open to the needs of an unprecedented situation in their supply chains and markets and the lives and environment of their employees. But, of course, if you were employed during the pandemic, different countries' governments made different financial arrangements for businesses and employees. Still, ultimately the pandemic put new challenges in front of executives and owners, placing demands on them as they would never have expected.

We know that in the case of businesses which have survived the pandemic and are on a trajectory of recovery will have learned skills which prepared them for the next disaster, which will also be known as unprecedented.

In the same way as above, resilient project delivery organisations have agile and empowered teams that can collaborate and make decisions quickly and independently. Leaders in the delivery functions are committed to continuous learning and improvement, encouraging innovation.

Resilient project teams have strong relationships and open internal and external communication channels. As a result, they are better equipped to manage risks, respond to challenges, and seize opportunities, which can help to achieve project objectives and, ultimately, intended outcomes.

Summarising resilient organisational factors

Clear and flexible strategy: Resilient organisations have a clear vision and strategy that is flexible enough to adapt to changing circumstances.

Strong leadership: Resilient organisations have strong and effective leaders who can guide the organisation through challenging times and make difficult decisions.

Robust and adaptable systems: Resilient organisations have systems and processes that are robust and adaptable, allowing them to respond quickly and effectively to unexpected events.

Agile and empowered teams: Resilient organisations have agile and empowered teams that can collaborate and make decisions quickly and independently.

Continuous learning and improvement: Resilient organisations are committed to continuous learning and improvement and encourage experimentation and innovation.

Strong relationships and communication: Resilient organisations have strong relationships and open communication channels, both internally and externally.

Positive Leadership in Project Delivery

The Project Management Institute (PMI.org) lists several critical leadership skills, sometimes incorrectly called soft skills. I say that they are misleadingly called soft skills because we are learning that the ability to use appropriate leadership and management skills in situations in the organisational context can make or break the organisation's sustainability. This makes leadership skills much less soft and far more critical. Skills necessary in the project delivery context are communication, problem-solving, time management, collaboration, emotional intelligence, negotiation, adaptability, critical thinking, and strategic thinking.

Effective communication is crucial for any project to succeed. It involves speaking and writing clearly and listening actively to others' ideas and feedback. Good communication helps ensure that everyone involved in the project knows their roles, responsibilities, and expectations. In addition, clear communication can help to avoid misunderstandings, conflicts, and delays in the project.

Project managers need to be able to lead their teams towards success. Effective leadership involves inspiring, motivating, and guiding team members towards achieving project goals. Leaders need to set a clear vision for the project, communicate that vision effectively, and ensure that everyone on the team is working towards the same goal. Effective leaders also need to be able to provide constructive feedback and recognition for good work.

Every project is likely to encounter some problems along the way. Project managers need to be able to identify issues, analyze them, and come up with practical solutions. Good problem-solving skills involve looking at situations from different perspectives, thinking creatively, and making decisions based on data and evidence.

Time management is essential in project management. Effective project managers need to be able to prioritize tasks, create schedules, and manage resources to meet project deadlines. Good time management helps ensure that the project stays on track and that team members work effectively and efficiently.

Projects often involve multiple stakeholders, both within and outside of the organization. Practical collaboration skills involve working effectively with others, including team members, stakeholders, and vendors. Collaboration skills involve communicating effectively, negotiating, and resolving conflicts that may arise during the project.

Emotional intelligence involves understanding and managing one's emotions and those of others. Effective project managers must build strong relationships with team members and stakeholders, which requires empathy, self-awareness, and social skills. Good emotional intelligence helps project managers to communicate effectively, manage conflict, and motivate team members.

Negotiation skills are essential in project management. Project managers need to be able to negotiate with stakeholders to ensure that project goals are aligned with organizational objectives. Good negotiation skills involve listening actively, understanding different perspectives, and finding solutions for everyone involved.

Projects often involve changes to requirements, resources, and schedules. Effective project managers need to be able to adapt to these changes and adjust project plans accordingly. Good adaptability skills involve thinking on your feet, being flexible, and adjusting plans quickly.

Critical thinking involves analysing information, identifying patterns, and making decisions based on data and evidence. Effective project managers must use critical thinking skills to assess risks, identify opportunities, and make decisions that benefit the project and the organization.

Strategic thinking involves thinking long-term and aligning project goals with organizational objectives. Effective project managers must see the big picture and understand how the project fits into the organization's overall strategy. Good strategic thinking helps project managers make decisions that align with the organization's objectives and deliver long-term benefits.

Here is a summary of the key leadership skills in the PMI Talent Triangle:

Communication: the ability to effectively communicate with stakeholders and team members.

Leadership: the ability to inspire and motivate team members to achieve project goals.

Problem-solving: the ability to identify and resolve issues that may arise during the project.

Time management: the ability to manage time effectively to meet project deadlines.

Collaboration: working effectively with others, including team members and stakeholders.

Emotional intelligence: the ability to understand and manage one's emotions and those of others.

Negotiation: the ability to negotiate effectively with stakeholders to achieve project goals.

Adaptability: the ability to be flexible and adapt to changes in project requirements or circumstances.

Critical thinking: the ability to analyze information and make decisions based on data and evidence.

Strategic thinking: thinking long-term and aligning project goals with organizational objectives.

Agile Organisations

Characteristics of agile organisations include:

Customer-centric focus

Cross-functional teams

Iterative and incremental development

Continuous learning and improvement

Flexibility and adaptability

Agile leadership

Organisational Agility

In today's rapidly changing business landscape, the ability of organizations to adapt quickly and effectively to new challenges and opportunities has become increasingly important. Agile organizations can respond quickly to changing market conditions, customer needs, and technological advancements. As a result, they are often better positioned to achieve long-term success.

Studying agile organizations can provide valuable insights into the strategies and practices that enable companies to remain competitive and innovative in a dynamic and complex environment. In addition, by understanding the factors contributing to agility, organizations can better prepare themselves for future disruptions and improve their ability to adapt to changing circumstances.

Furthermore, examining agile organizations can also inform best practices for leaders and managers, helping them to develop the skills and competencies necessary to build an agile culture within their organizations.

In addition, agile organizations are often more collaborative and customer-centric, leading to better outcomes for the organization and its stakeholders. Organizations can build stronger relationships with their customers, suppliers, and partners by fostering agility and increasing trust and loyalty.

Agile and Resilient definitions overlap significantly but do not replace each other in description. Therefore, we will list them separately but allow the overlap to be self-evident.

Agile organisations can respond quickly and effectively to changing circumstances and customer needs. They are characterised by their ability to be flexible, adaptive, and innovative in their approach to business. These organisations typically embrace values and principles that emphasise collaboration, experimentation, continuous learning, and rapid feedback.

Agile organisations deliver value to their customers and prioritise customer needs in their decision-making processes. Agile organisations prefer to work in cross-functional teams, which are empowered to make decisions and deliver results independently. They use an iterative and incremental approach to projects and product development, breaking work into small chunks and delivering value in short cycles.

Agile organisations prioritise continuous learning and improvement, gathering feedback and data to inform decision-making and drive innovation. For these reasons, they adapt quickly to changing circumstances and are comfortable with ambiguity and uncertainty. This attitude requires 'Agile' leaders who can create a culture of agility, promote collaboration and innovation, and empower their teams to make decisions and take action.

Agile organisations are better equipped to respond to the rapidly changing business environment, innovate in their approach to business, and deliver value to their customers quickly and efficiently.

Understanding why organizations are agile is crucial for individual organizations, the broader business community, and society. By fostering agility, organizations can better navigate uncertainty and contribute to the resilience of the broader ecosystem in which they operate.

Summarising agile organisations

Customer-centric focus: Agile organisations deliver value to their customers and prioritise customer needs in their decision-making processes.

Cross-functional teams: Agile organisations work in cross-functional teams, which are empowered to make decisions and deliver results independently.

Iterative and incremental development: Agile organisations use an iterative and incremental approach to development.

Continuous learning and improvement: Agile organisations prioritise continuous learning and improvement.

Flexibility and adaptability: Agile organisations are comfortable with ambiguity and uncertainty.

Agile leadership: Agile organisations are led by agile leaders who empower their teams to make decisions and take action.

Part 2
Building healthy team cultures

Key differences between project teams and regular teams:

Temporary vs Ongoing

Cross-Functional vs Specialised

Defined Objectives vs Ongoing Goals

Limited Resources vs Sustained Resources

Agile vs Hierarchical

Risk Management vs Stability

The importance of understanding teams

In the modern workplace, teams are a fundamental unit of organizational structure, with individuals coming together to work collaboratively towards shared goals. While there are many types of teams, two common forms are regular and project teams.

Regular teams are long-standing groups of individuals who work together continuously to accomplish a particular function within the organization. On the other hand, project teams are formed for a specific purpose, usually with a defined timeframe, to accomplish a particular project or initiative.

Understanding the differences between project and regular teams is vital for organizations as it can impact how work is planned, executed and managed. Project teams require different skill sets, processes, and tools than regular teams, requiring a different approach to leadership and management.

The difference between project teams and regular teams

Project teams are typically assembled from individuals with specific skills and experience to work on a particular project. Once the project is completed, the team is typically disbanded, and members return to their regular roles within the organization. In contrast, regular teams are ongoing and work together to achieve ongoing business objectives.

There are several key differences between project teams and regular teams:

Temporary vs Ongoing: Project teams are typically formed for a specific project or initiative and are disbanded once the project is completed. In contrast, regular teams are ongoing and work together continuously.

Cross-Functional vs Specialised: Project teams are typically cross-functional, consisting of individuals with diverse skills and expertise required for the specific project. Conversely, regular teams often comprise individuals with similar or complementary skills and expertise.

Defined Objectives vs Ongoing Goals: Project teams have a defined set of objectives to accomplish within a specific timeframe. In contrast, regular teams often have ongoing goals and objectives that are continually refined and adjusted over time.

Limited Resources vs Sustained Resources: Project teams often work within limited resources, including time, budget, and personnel, while regular teams typically have more sustained resources to support their ongoing work.

Agile vs Hierarchical: Project teams are often structured in an agile manner, with a more fluid hierarchy and decision-making process, while regular teams are often structured hierarchically, with clear lines of authority and decision-making processes.

Risk Management vs Stability: Project teams typically focus more on risk management and mitigation, as the project represents a more significant investment of time, resources, and budget, while regular teams often focus on maintaining stability and efficiency in ongoing operations.

In summary, project teams are typically formed for a specific, time-limited project requiring diverse skills and expertise. In contrast, regular teams are ongoing and often composed of individuals with similar or complementary skills and expertise. In addition, project teams often work within limited resources, have defined objectives, and are structured agilely, focusing on risk management and mitigation.

Therefore, understanding the difference between project teams and regular teams is essential for managers and leaders as it allows them to design and implement appropriate processes, tools and leadership approaches that match the specific needs of each type of team. By doing so, organizations can improve their efficiency and effectiveness, enhance collaboration, and ultimately achieve their goals.

"I believe that trust is crucial in building a successful team. You have to be honest, transparent and clear in your communication and make sure your players feel supported and empowered." Sarina Wiegman

Traits of a psychologically safe project team:

Open communication

Constructive feedback

Trust

Collaboration

Support

Psychological safety in delivery teams

Psychological safety refers to individuals' perception that they can express themselves without fear of negative consequences, such as rejection or ridicule. In project teams, psychological safety is critical to team performance and success.

Psychologically safe project teams are those in which team members feel comfortable sharing their thoughts, ideas, and concerns without fear of negative consequences. They feel their contributions are valued, and they can make mistakes without punishment. This creates an environment where team members are more likely to take risks, be creative, and share their knowledge and expertise.

The following traits can characterise a psychologically safe project team:

Open communication: Team members are comfortable speaking their minds and are unafraid to express their thoughts, opinions, and concerns.

Constructive feedback: Feedback is given and received constructively and respectfully, emphasising learning and growth rather than blame or punishment.

Trust: Team members trust one another to do their job effectively and efficiently and to collaborate effectively.

Collaboration: Team members work effectively and collaboratively to achieve project goals, focusing on the team's success.

Support: Team members support one another and will provide help and resources when needed.

Project teams can achieve better performance and outcomes by creating a psychologically safe environment. As a result, team members are more likely to take risks, be innovative, and share their knowledge and expertise, which can lead to improved decision-making, higher-quality work, and increased efficiency. Additionally, team members are more likely to be engaged and committed to the project, which can lead to increased job satisfaction and retention.

"I've learned that everything you do in rugby, you do it as a team. If you don't have the support of your teammates, you can't achieve anything. You have to work together, you have to trust each other, and you have to have each other's backs."

Siya Kolisi

Creating a psychologically safe project team:

Lead by example

Encourage open communication

Create a culture of trust

Provide psychological safety training

Foster team cohesion

Celebrate diversity

Avoid blaming or shaming

Creating psychologically safe project teams

Psychologically safe teams are those in which team members feel comfortable sharing their thoughts, ideas, and concerns without fear of negative consequences.

Creating a psychologically safe project team requires a deliberate effort by team leaders and members to establish an environment where everyone feels comfortable expressing themselves without fear of negative consequences. Here are some ways to create a psychologically safe project team:

Lead by example: As a team leader, model the behaviour you want to see in your team. Share your thoughts, ideas, and concerns, and be open to feedback and constructive criticism.

Encourage open communication: Set the tone for open communication by creating opportunities for team members to share their thoughts and ideas. Encourage active listening, and respond with respect and empathy to feedback.

Create a culture of trust: Build trust by being honest and transparent with your team. Encourage your team members to be open and honest with one another, and work to resolve conflicts constructively and respectfully.

Provide psychological safety training: Training team members on the importance of psychological safety and creating a psychologically safe environment. This can include effective communication, active listening, and conflict resolution training.

Foster team cohesion: Create opportunities for team members to get to know one another personally. This can include team-building activities or social events that allow team members to connect and build relationships.

Celebrate diversity: Encourage team members to bring their unique perspectives and experiences to the table. Celebrate diversity and create an environment that values differences.

Avoid blaming or shaming: Avoid blaming or shaming team members for mistakes or failures. Instead, focus on solutions and use mistakes as learning opportunities.

By focusing on these strategies, you can create a psychologically safe project team where team members feel comfortable sharing their thoughts, ideas, and concerns without fear of negative consequences. This can lead to better communication, higher quality work, and improved outcomes for the project.

***

Because our focus in this book is creating a resilient and sustainable project delivery culture, we should consider in the following chapters what causes anxiety within your project management community and can even result in higher attrition rates and difficulty hiring people into your organisation.

Let's consider some of the common fears that project managers sometimes experience.

Project Managers' fears

Common project managers' fears:

Becoming Obsolete

Lack of Advancement Opportunities

Losing Control

Inadequate Resources

Failing to Deliver

Burnout

Difficulty Balancing Work and Life

What are project managers' career fears?

Project managers may have a variety of career fears related to their profession. It is helpful to explore some of those reasons here because this book aims to reduce project managers' fears and create a constructive environment where they can initiate, plan, execute, and deliver the projects and products your organisation needs. For example, suppose they have constant anxiety over their future within the organisation or their industry. In that case, you may not find people stepping up to projects in your area, or you may find that they hold back on bad news or leave you to what they believe is a safer environment, even if it is not a more financially viable environment.

Project managers may fear their skills and experience becoming outdated, particularly in light of emerging technologies and changing business practices. They may fear limited opportunities for advancement within their organisation or in the project management profession, potentially limiting their career growth and earning potential.

Project managers may fear losing control of their projects, particularly if they are working with stakeholders who are unresponsive or resistant to change. Their fears will be compounded if they feel they will not have the resources to deliver projects successfully, particularly in light of limited budgets or staffing constraints. They may fear failing to deliver projects on time, within budget, and to the required quality standards, potentially damaging their professional reputation and career prospects.

Project managers may fear that they will experience burnout, particularly if they are working on multiple projects simultaneously or facing significant workload pressures. And fear they will struggle to balance their work and personal lives, potentially leading to stress, health issues, and reduced job satisfaction.

To summarise project managers' anxieties, they may fear:

Becoming Obsolete: Project managers may fear their skills and experience becoming outdated.

Lack of Advancement Opportunities: Project managers may fear limited opportunities for advancement.

Losing Control: Project managers may fear losing control of their projects.

Inadequate Resources: Project managers may fear they will not have the resources to deliver projects successfully.

Failing to Deliver: Project managers may fear that they will fail to deliver projects within the constraints damaging their professional reputation.

Burnout: Project managers may fear that they will experience burnout.

Difficulty Balancing Work and Life: Project managers may fear that they will struggle to balance their work and personal lives.

Overall, project managers may experience a range of career fears related to their profession and may take steps to mitigate these risks through ongoing professional development, effective communication, stakeholder engagement, and self-care.

**

Beyond this list of project management fears are some reasons project managers will resign from your organisation or at least transfer to another part of your company. Common to the list above and the reasons for resignation are the poor work-life balance and a lack of career advancement opportunities.

Referring to the list of fears and anxieties, and again that the purpose of this book is to create a resilient project management delivery culture, it is worth looking at some examples of why project managers would leave your organisation.

Reasons project managers leave your organisation:

Poor communication

Unrealistic expectations

Lack of support

Poor work-life balance

Conflicts with team members or stakeholders

Lack of career growth opportunities

What causes project managers to resign?

Many factors can cause project managers to resign from their positions. For example, project managers may resign if they feel there is no room for growth or advancement in their current position or organisation or some of the following:

A lack of effective communication is a common reason project managers resign. Suppose team members, stakeholders, or executives are not communicating effectively. In that case, the project manager may feel frustrated or overwhelmed, leading to burnout and a desire to leave the position. If their work-life balance becomes too skewed in favour of work, the project manager may feel burnt out and decide to resign.

If project managers are given unrealistic expectations or timelines, they may feel they are being set up for failure. This suspicion can cause stress and anxiety and may lead to a decision to resign. In addition, project managers require support from team members, stakeholders, and executives to be successful. If the project manager feels they are not receiving the support they need, they may become frustrated and demotivated.

Conflict is a natural part of any project. Still, if it becomes too frequent or intense, it can cause the manager to feel overwhelmed and ineffective. If the conflicts cannot be resolved, the project manager may feel that resigning is best.

Common reasons project managers may leave the organisation:

Poor communication: A lack of effective communication is a common reason project managers resign.

Unrealistic expectations: If project managers are given unrealistic expectations or timelines, they may feel they are being set up for failure.

Lack of support: Project managers require support from team members, stakeholders, and executives to be successful.

Poor work-life balance: Project managers often work long hours and are under significant stress

Conflicts with team members or stakeholders: Conflict is a natural part of any project, but if it becomes too frequent or intense, it can cause the project manager to feel overwhelmed and ineffective.

Lack of career growth opportunities: Project managers may resign if they feel there is no room for growth or advancement in their current position or organisation.

These are just a few of the factors that can cause project managers to resign. Effective communication, clear expectations, strong support networks, and a healthy work-life balance are all essential for retaining skilled project managers and ensuring project success.

Your organisation and the project board must support the delivery function in creating a healthy climate where project management fears and concerns are surfaced and dealt with appropriately.

Building a healthy team climate

Build trust

Foster positive relationships

Set clear expectations

Encourage collaboration

Recognise achievements

Encourage feedback

Support development

Manage conflicts

Emphasise work-life balance

Creating a healthy project and team climate

Creating a healthy team climate requires deliberate efforts by team leaders and members to foster an environment where everyone feels valued, respected, and supported. Here are some strategies to create a healthy team climate:

Build trust: Building trust is essential for creating a healthy team climate. Encourage open communication, support team members, and lead by example to foster a culture of trust.

Foster positive relationships: Encourage team members to build positive relationships with one another. This can be done through team-building activities or social events that allow team members to connect and build relationships.

Set clear expectations: Establish expectations for how team members should work together. This practice can include guidelines for communication, collaboration, and conflict resolution.

Encourage collaboration: Foster a collaborative environment where team members work together to achieve shared goals. Encourage team members to share their ideas and expertise to find the best solutions.

Recognise achievements: Recognise and celebrate achievements by team members. This recognition can be done through public recognition, rewards, or other forms of appreciation.

Encourage feedback: Encourage team members to provide feedback to one another. This can be done through regular performance reviews or anonymous feedback channels.

Support development: Provide opportunities for team members to develop their skills and knowledge. These opportunities can include training, mentorship, or other forms of professional development.

Manage conflicts: Address conflicts as soon as they arise. Encourage team members to work together to find a constructive and respectful solution.

Emphasise work-life balance: Encourage team members to achieve a healthy work-life balance. This can be done by offering flexible working arrangements or providing resources to help team members manage their workload.

By focusing on these strategies, you can create a healthy team climate where team members feel valued, respected, and supported. This can lead to improved team morale, higher quality work, and better outcomes for the project.

Project health

Some key project health measures may include:

Schedule performance

Budget performance

Risk management

Quality management

Stakeholder satisfaction

Team performance

Key project health measures

Key project health measures are metrics used to evaluate a project's overall health and performance. These metrics provide insight into critical areas of the project, such as progress, risk, quality, and stakeholder satisfaction, which can be used to identify areas for improvement and make data-driven decisions.

Progress management assesses whether the project is on track to meet its scheduled completion date. It includes metrics such as planned vs actual start and end dates, task completion rates, and milestones achieved. Similarly, financial health tracking assesses whether the project stays within its budget. It tracks metrics such as planned vs actual costs, cost variance, and earned value.

Risk Management assesses how well risks are identified, analysed, and managed throughout the project. It includes metrics such as risk identification and prioritisation, risk mitigation strategies, and risk monitoring and control.

Project Quality assurance assesses whether the project meets its quality objectives, including metrics such as defects found, defects fixed, and customer satisfaction with the quality of the deliverables.

Stakeholder and Communications management assess the level of satisfaction of project stakeholders, including customers, sponsors, and team members, using metrics such as stakeholder feedback, surveys, engagement, and communication.

Team performance and motivation is a critical measure assessing the overall performance and productivity of the project team. It includes team morale and satisfaction, communication, and velocity metrics.

By tracking these key project health measures, project managers and stakeholders can gain a comprehensive view of the project's performance, identify areas for improvement, and make data-driven decisions to improve the project's overall health and success.

Summarising key project health measures

Schedule performance: This measure assesses whether the project is on track to meet its scheduled completion date.

Budget performance: This measure assesses whether the project stays within its budget.

Risk management: This measure assesses how well risks are identified, analysed, and managed throughout the project.

Quality management: This measure assesses whether the project meets its quality objectives.

Stakeholder satisfaction: This measure assesses the level of satisfaction of project stakeholders, including customers, sponsors, and team members.

Team performance: This measure assesses the overall performance and productivity of the project team.

Troubled projects

Several signs may indicate a troubled project. Some of the most common signs include:

Scope creep

Quality issues

Budget overruns

Missed deadlines

Unresolved conflicts

Lack of communication

High turnover or absenteeism

Constantly changing requirements

What are the signs of a troubled project?

One of the most apparent signs of a troubled project is when tasks are not completed on time or deadlines are consistently missed. In addition, when the project exceeds its budget or requires additional funds, it may be a sign that it is not being managed effectively.

If the project scope continually expands, it may be a sign that the project is not managed correctly, and there may be insufficient planning or poor communication. Changes in project requirements may be necessary, but excessive changes can indicate a lack of proper planning, communication, or understanding of project objectives.

A lack of effective communication between team members, stakeholders, or project sponsors may lead to misunderstandings, delays, and poor decision-making.

Suppose team members frequently miss work or quit the project. In that case, it may indicate poor team morale, inadequate project management, or misaligned expectations. This poor morale can impact product quality. Furthermore, unresolved team conflict can lead to poor collaboration, decreased productivity, and a negative impact on project outcomes.

When project deliverables are consistently poor, it may indicate a lack of attention to detail or inadequate quality control processes.

Summarising troubled project indicators

Missed deadlines: Tasks are not completed on time, or deadlines are consistently missed.

Budget overruns: The project exceeds its budget or requires additional funds.

Scope creep: The project scope continually expands.

Lack of communication: A lack of effective communication between team members, stakeholders, or project sponsors.

High turnover or absenteeism: Team members frequently miss work or quit the project.

Quality issues: When project deliverables are consistently poor.

Constantly changing requirements: Excessive changes can indicate a lack of proper planning, communication, or understanding of project objectives.

Unresolved conflicts: When project team members have unresolved conflicts, it can lead to poor collaboration, decreased productivity, and a negative impact on project outcomes.

Identifying these signs of a troubled project early on can help project managers take corrective actions to get the project back on track and ensure its success.

***

Key to our resilient project delivery culture is the influential role of the project board, led by the Senior Responsible Owner (SRO), also known as the Project Sponsor.

Let's look at the levers the project board has in our resilient culture.

Project board leadership levers:

Vision and strategy

Risk management

Resource allocation

Stakeholder management

Governance and oversight

Communication and Collaboration

Key project board leadership levers

Project board leadership levers refer to the key levers that project board members can use to influence and guide a project's overall direction, success, and outcomes. These levers are critical to ensuring that the project is aligned with the organisation's objectives, that risks are effectively managed, and that stakeholder expectations are met.

As we have said elsewhere in the book, we cannot discuss creating a resilient or positive project delivery culture without discussing the project board and its contribution to the culture and climate within a project. This is important because a project board manifests, to a certain extent, the overall project delivery culture. However, we accept that not every project sponsor or board chairperson represents the culture well. However, we do remember that the project board is not made up of only people from your organisation, but the senior responsible owner, usually from the commissioning executive, a senior user and at least one senior supplier, and possibly other key stakeholders.

In projects where the roles and responsibilities of the board and the different board members are clearly defined, you have a greater chance of cascading the positive culture down to the project manager. This is because one of the ground rules of a project board directing a project correctly is that the final arbiter of decisions is the SRO. The project board should be available to the project manager on an ad hoc basis; specifically, each board member is available for ad hoc consultation and guidance of the project manager for their area of expertise or experience.

Project board members must have a clear vision and strategy for the project and ensure that the project is aligned with the organisation's overall objectives and strategy. This includes setting clear goals and objectives for the project, defining the scope and boundaries of the project, and establishing a roadmap for the project's execution.

The board members must effectively monitor strategic risks associated with the project and support the project manager in any risk response and mitigation planning. This includes assessing and monitoring the likelihood and impact of these risks and developing strategies with the project manager to mitigate or avoid these risks.

Project board members must ensure that the project has the necessary resources to be successful, including funding, personnel, and equipment. They must prioritise these resources and allocate them in a way that maximises project success.

The board must effectively manage stakeholder expectations and engagement throughout the project lifecycle. This includes participating in stakeholder identification, understanding their needs and expectations, and communicating with them throughout the project.

The project board must establish a governance framework and oversight processes to manage the project effectively and efficiently. This includes defining roles and responsibilities, establishing decision-making processes, and monitoring project performance against established metrics.

Project board members must foster a culture of open communication and collaboration among project stakeholders. This includes promoting transparency, creating opportunities for feedback and input, and encouraging collaboration among project team members.

Summarising some project board responsibilities that support the project manager:

Vision and strategy: Project board members must have a clear vision and strategy for the project and must ensure that the project is aligned with the organisation's overall objectives and strategy.

Risk management: Project board members must participate in risk management as some become high risk, high impact, and close proximity.

Resource allocation: Project board members must ensure that the project has the necessary resources to be successful.

Stakeholder management: Project board members must effectively manage stakeholder expectations and engagement throughout the project lifecycle.

Governance and oversight: Project board members must establish a governance framework and oversight processes to ensure the project is managed effectively and efficiently.

Communication and collaboration: Project board members must foster a culture of open communication and collaboration among project stakeholders.

By effectively using these project board leadership levers, project board members can help ensure the project's success, manage risks, respond rapidly to escalations, support the project manager, and ensure the project delivers value to stakeholders.

Part 3
The E4Xchange Leadership Model

Implementing change with the E4 Xchange Leadership Model

The E4 Xchange Leadership Model™ (E4XLM™) is a sound framework for organisational change leadership at scale. The E4 Xchange Leadership Model incorporates the models of the leading thinkers in large-scale enterprise transformation. The model does not profess to change the landscape in terms of theory; however, it makes the concepts of change leadership more understandable and, therefore, implementable in your organisation. Because it starts with several fundamental principles and incorporates the thinking of leading practitioners and academics, it can be introduced in low-level change and scaled at an enterprise level. The nature of the model is that it is cyclical and is a virtuous cycle and not a static set of rules. The four major model categories can be evolved or unpacked to include the appropriate organisational change steps to meet the situation's needs.

The letter X is commonly an abbreviation for transformation. Still, it is also widely used as a phrase reflecting multiples of change or step levels of change. Many have heard that changing something in our organisation or business will impact 2x or 3x, or 4x, where 'x' is a multiplier. The 'x' indicates the scalability and possible exponential growth resulting from a change model. The E4 Xchange Leadership Model TM provides a convenient set of hooks to locate the practice that your organisational model will implement.

We often refer to the senior leadership level as the CXO, with X as a specific designation. For example, CEO for Chief Executive Officer or CDO (Chief Data Officer) or CPO (Chief People Officer, and so on. In this case, we indicate that transformational change comes from the top of the organisation and the relevant department heads.

X is also for transformation. However, in our model, the transformation is not static and is not a one-time-only case. Instead, it is an ongoing cycle in this new era, particularly in the lessons learned from responding to the COVID-19 pandemic of 2020 to 2022.

Employee Engagement Opportunities™

If we take the E4XLM down four levels, we see how it applies at each leadership and impact level. There are four primary levels at which the enterprise engages with its employees:

Enterprise Leadership sets strategy and direction as an Executive and has responsibility for casting the vision and modelling the culture. Divisions or Departments are Teams of Teams. They interpret, manage, communicate and lead their reportees, individuals and team leaders.

Teams deliver the products and services of the organisation. Team leaders manage and lead their groups and individuals to high performance. Individuals are leaders by role or behaviour and are employees with their careers and aspirations.

Although the terminology varies, all established change models speak about communicating compelling reasons for change. The models discuss drawing in other believers who will champion the vision and share the change with all stakeholders, including employees. They create the desire, motivation, and confidence to embrace the change. Engagement with the organisation or team is where the E4 Xchange Leadership Model starts. Whatever the level of leadership sponsoring and driving the change is where you have the first steps of engagement with your organisation. E4XLM has four high-level steps. These are engagement with people, Enabling people, Encouraging, and Evaluating progress.

Evaluation and engagement are closely linked. It is an artificial distinction, but evaluation of statistics and performance needs to happen to some degree before formally engaging the results with the individuals or teams where you surface areas to adjust and enable. Each of these four main elements is the top level of several possible tools in a toolbox designed around your organisational culture and lessons learned from previous changes and best practices you may have in-house or procure from outside consultants.

You will realise that the engagement or the E4XLM follows from the strategy and planning and does not profess to be the strategic planning tool. You will have used many different organisations and methodologies to crystallise your vision and define the goals and objectives that drive your change programme. E4XLM provides the framework for engaging and enabling your leadership team and then for you to encourage or, more specifically, give courage and empower your leaders below you or your team to execute the plan with regular evaluation.

The model starts with Engagement.

Employee Engagement is one of any organisation's key objectives. Employees engaged in their work and the organisation produce their best work and build their peers and organisation.

Engaged employees are fully committed to their work and the goals of the organization they work for. As a result, they feel a sense of ownership and responsibility towards their work. As a result, they are motivated to give their best effort.

Some signs of an engaged employee include being proactive, taking the initiative to get their work done, contributing to the team, being passionate about their work, and finding meaning in what they do.

They have positive attitudes and are willing to help others, going the extra mile to meet deadlines and exceed expectations. They welcome feedback and are willing to learn and grow.

Engaging with your team means ensuring they understand their roles and responsibilities and how their work contributes to the organisation's goals. Offer them appropriate training and development programs to help build their skills and advance their careers.

Create a positive and supportive team environment where employees feel valued and included. Provide them with regular feedback and communicate openly about the state of the organization and their role in it.

Celebrate achievements and acknowledge when employees go above and beyond.

By implementing these strategies, organisations can help employees feel engaged and motivated to do their best work.

A people-centric approach

You will notice that the E4 Xchange Leadership Model is people-centric, action-oriented, performance-driven, and agile.

At the centre of the X in Xchange are people. Engagement, Enablement, Encouragement, and Evaluation ultimately intersect at the individual level of the organisation.

The well-known Toyota production system also has people at the centre of what they call the TPS house. Apart from all the process-related improvements, they put training at the centre of their strategy. Training to develop the people and the teams to improve the production processes consistently. Doing this reinforces a strong and stable culture well known within the Japanese worldview. This Toyota production system involves cross-functional teams and teaches individuals to work together. This consistent engagement, equipping, and encouragement of people empowers the teams to improve.

If we have learned nothing else in the two years of the pandemic, we have learned the importance and impact on people of accelerated and perpetual change. Before the pandemic, the phrase had arisen that change is the only constant. This phrase was thrown around lightly and with much truth behind it. We have discovered our extraordinary ability to cope with change in the face of crisis and now as we enter the new era of work. We must be mindful of the stress of such change and how the most people-centric reaction or response was the secret sauce of staff motivation and retention during the most challenging times.

Engagement, Enablement, and Encouragement are people-centred leadership behaviours. These modes of leadership foster the employees' feelings of engagement with their work, teams, and organisation. It is widely acknowledged that people do not leave organisations; they leave managers.

Evaluation is a management task – measuring performance against goals. Evaluation can result in the need for corrective action at a team or employee level. This is how the Engagement behaviour coaches, motivates, rewards, or corrects, as appropriate.

It is action-oriented.

Engagement combines active listening, intentional affirmation, constructive conversations, vision-casting, coaching, mentoring, correcting and directing. It is these and more. Therefore, engagement aims to create an environment for growth, performance, initiative, ambition, and commitment to the organisation's strategic goals.

Enablement provides the appropriate tools, knowledge, structures, processes, and experience to correct or enhance the ability to perform one's duties. This provision is a result of Evaluation and Engagement.

It is performance-driven.

Encouragement is to 'give courage'. You have given appropriate support and enablement for effective performance and delivery to agreed and expected standards. This encouragement incorporates empowerment, clear expectation, exhortation and, in the case of managed performance, evaluation more regularly than consistent performers.

It is agile.

E4XLM is a developmental way of leading for managers, leaders, and team members. It is a wheel of leadership habits in perpetual motion. It is as applicable to Agile Scrums, sprints, iterations, and incremental delivery of products, as it is to leading people and teams in business, as usual, change and transformation management, and project human resource management.

E4XLM – Implementing your change

Let us look at implementing your playbook with the four main elements of the E4XLM life cycle.

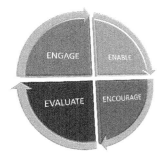

Engage

Remember, creating change is a process that takes time and effort. In addition, engaging with employees and creating a culture of change requires consistent communication, transparency, and trust. Following these steps can increase the likelihood of success in creating change within your organisation.

Start by communicating the vision and goals of the change you want to create. This communication helps employees understand the purpose of the change and its potential benefits. It also helps create a shared understanding and ownership of the change.

Involve employees in the change process by asking for their input and feedback. This participation helps to increase their sense of ownership and engagement in the change.

Create a culture of transparency and trust by being open and honest with employees about the change process, including any challenges or setbacks. This transparency helps build trust and credibility, which can increase employee buy-in.

Encouraging openness and honesty in your teams:

Set clear expectations

Foster a collaborative environment

Provide regular opportunities for communication

Listen actively

Encourage feedback

Address conflicts immediately

Promote mutual respect

Engaging with openness and honesty

Encouraging your team members to be open and honest with one another, and work to resolve conflicts constructively and respectfully, is an essential part of creating a psychologically safe project team. Here are some ways to encourage this behaviour:

When team members express their thoughts or concerns, listen to them. Demonstrate that you take their feedback seriously and are willing to work with them to find a solution.

Make it clear to your team that open and honest communication is expected and valued. Let the team know that it is encouraged to express thoughts and ideas and that constructive feedback is always welcome. This means promoting a team-oriented culture where everyone's contributions are valued.

Provide regular opportunities for team members to communicate with one another. This can include team meetings, one-on-one meetings, or informal communication channels like chat or email.

When conflicts do arise, address them immediately. Then, encourage team members to work together to find a constructive and respectful solution.

Ensure that all team members show mutual respect to one another. This means avoiding negative behaviours like gossiping or speaking negatively about others.

By following these strategies, you can encourage your team members to be open and honest with one another and work to resolve conflicts constructively and respectfully. This can help create a psychologically safe project team that is more productive, efficient, and ultimately successful.

What motivates us?

When we look at this E4 model, we should pause to look at what motivates and demotivates your colleagues and peers within the organisation. Of course, people come to work for many reasons, the most fundamental being the need to provide for themselves and their families financially. Still, as soon as they have met that baseline, their motivations and demotivators start to move along a spectrum or progression of wants and needs.

Here are ten common motivators:

Recognition and appreciation: People are often motivated by being recognized and appreciated for their contributions and accomplishments. This can take the form of public praise or rewards.

Autonomy: People value the ability to work independently and make decisions. Autonomy can also provide a sense of ownership and accountability.

Growth and development: Many people are motivated by opportunities to learn new skills and grow in their careers. Organizations that offer training, mentorship, and advancement opportunities can be very appealing.

Purpose: People are often motivated by a sense of purpose and connection to a larger mission. They want to feel that their work is meaningful and contributes to something important.

Challenge: People motivated by challenges thrive on complex tasks and goals that require them to stretch beyond their comfort zones.

Responsibility: People motivated by responsibility want to take on leadership roles and have a sense of ownership over their work.

Flexibility: People value flexibility in their work arrangements, such as working remotely or adjusting their hours.

Compensation and benefits: While money isn't always the most important motivator, people want to be fairly compensated for their work and access benefits like health insurance and retirement savings plans.

Social connection: Many people are motivated by social connections and enjoy working with colleagues they respect and admire.

Work-life balance: People want to feel like they have a healthy balance between work and personal lives. Organizations that prioritize work-life balance can be desirable to employees.

What demotivates us?

The top demotivators in the workplace may vary depending on individual circumstances and organizational culture. However, here are some common demotivators that can negatively impact employee engagement and productivity:

Lack of recognition: Employees may feel demotivated when their supervisors or colleagues do not acknowledge or appreciate their efforts.

Poor leadership: Employees may be demotivated by ineffective or abusive managers who fail to provide clear direction or support.

Micromanagement: Employees may feel demotivated when constantly monitored or given limited autonomy in their work.

Lack of growth opportunities: Employees may be demotivated when they feel stuck in their current role with limited opportunities for advancement or professional development.

Unfair compensation: When employees perceive their pay or benefits as unfair compared to their peers or industry standards.

Toxic culture: As mentioned elsewhere, employees are demotivated when the workplace culture is harmful or toxic, characterized by bullying, harassment, or discrimination.

Inadequate resources: It is hard to be motivated when you feel set up for failure by lacking the necessary tools, technology, or resources to perform your job effectively.

Unclear expectations: Uncertainty about job expectations and your job responsibilities leads to confusion or frustration.

Lack of trust: Employees may be demotivated when they feel their colleagues or supervisors do not trust or respect their work.

Burnout: Overwork or stress leads to exhaustion or reduced engagement.

Employers must address these demotivators and create a positive work environment fostering employee engagement, productivity, and well-being.

Enable

Project management enablement involves providing the tools, resources, and support needed to ensure the success of project managers and their teams. Here are some project management enablement strategies:

Provide employees with the training and resources they need to successfully implement the change and help them develop the skills and expertise needed to manage projects successfully. This enablement can include training on new systems, processes, project management methodologies, software tools, and best practices.

Standardise project management processes to ensure consistency and efficiency across projects. This standardisation can include developing standard templates for project plans, timelines, and deliverables.

Provide project managers and team members access to project management tools, such as project management software, collaboration tools, and document management systems. This access to tools helps to streamline project management and enhance communication and collaboration.

Define clear roles and responsibilities for project managers and team members to ensure everyone understands their responsibilities and expectations.

Establish clear communication channels to ensure project managers and team members communicate effectively and efficiently. These channels can include regular project meetings, status updates, and communication plans.

By implementing these project management enablement strategies, you can help project managers and their teams to work more efficiently, effectively, and collaboratively, ultimately improving the success of your projects.

Summarising project management enablement strategies

Provide training and resources: Provide employees with the training and resources they need to successfully implement the change and help them develop the skills and expertise needed to manage projects successfully.

Standardise project management processes: Standardise project management processes to ensure consistency and efficiency across projects.

Provide access to project management tools: Provide project managers and team members with access to project management tools.

Define clear roles and responsibilities: Define clear roles and responsibilities for project managers and team members to ensure that everyone understands their responsibilities and the expectations for their roles.

Establish clear communication channels: Establish clear communication channels to ensure that project managers and team members can communicate effectively and efficiently.

By implementing these project management enablement strategies, you can help project managers and their teams to work more efficiently, effectively, and collaboratively, ultimately improving the success of your projects.

Encourage and Empower

To Encourage is to 'Give Courage'.

Encouraging staff in your organisation means giving them the courage to do their job and taking calculated risks knowing you have their back. For example, project managers and team members need to know that you will give them air cover when they take a stand which protects the project schedule, budget, or product quality and, therefore, the outcomes anticipated in the business case.

Let us look for a moment at what employees fear and then at what we, as leaders, can do to create a resilient workforce in our project delivery environment.

What do employees fear in an organisation?

The top fears of employees in an organization may vary depending on individual circumstances and organizational culture. However, here are some common fears that employees may have.

Employees may fear losing their jobs due to layoffs, downsizing, or company restructuring. In addition, they may fear changes in the workplace, such as changes in job duties, new management, or new technology. This is compounded when they fear making mistakes or failing to meet expectations, leading to negative consequences such as demotions, job loss, or damaged reputations.

Your employee may feel anxious when they perceive a lack of control over their work environment, such as changes in policies, procedures, or management decisions. In addition, they may be afraid of not knowing what to expect in the future, such as not knowing their job responsibilities or the company's plans.

Your reportees may fear conflict with colleagues or managers, such as disagreements over work assignments or performance evaluations. In the same sense, they may fear being rejected or criticized by their peers or managers, leading to feelings of isolation or low self-esteem. This rejection may be discrimination based on race, gender, age, sexual orientation, or other personal characteristics.

Employees who are overworked and stressed may overcompensate in an uncertain work environment and may then be afraid of burning out due to long hours, high-stress levels, or an unsustainable workload, which can negatively impact their health, well-being, and productivity.

What can be done to 'give courage'?

Encourage open communication with employees about the organization's plans and reassure them of their job security. Provide clear expectations and goals for employees to help them focus on their work performance. Consider offering training and development opportunities to help employees expand their skill sets and make them more valuable to the organization.

Encourage a growth mindset, where mistakes are seen as opportunities for learning and improvement. Provide regular feedback and recognition to help employees feel valued and motivated. Create a supportive work environment that encourages risk-taking and experimentation.

Communicate clearly and frequently with employees about upcoming changes, providing as much information as possible. Consider offering training or support to help employees adjust to new systems or processes. Emphasize the potential benefits of the changes to help employees see the bigger picture.

Encourage employee involvement in decision-making processes and provide opportunities for input and feedback. Provide clear guidelines and expectations to help employees feel more in control of their work. Consider offering training or support to help employees develop coping strategies for dealing with change or uncertainty.

Provide regular updates and communication to help employees feel informed and engaged. Encourage employees to ask questions and seek clarification when needed. Foster a culture of adaptability and resilience to help employees feel prepared for unexpected changes.

Encourage open communication and active listening to help employees address conflicts constructively. Provide clear policies and procedures for conflict resolution. Offer mediation or coaching to help employees work through conflicts.

Provide regular feedback and recognition to help employees feel valued and motivated. Encourage a supportive work environment that emphasizes teamwork and collaboration. Offer training or support to help employees build resilience and cope with rejection.

Foster a culture of inclusion and diversity by promoting awareness and education around different identities and experiences. Develop policies and procedures for addressing discrimination and harassment. Provide training and support for managers and supervisors to help them recognize and address discriminatory behaviour.

Encourage work-life balance by promoting flexible work arrangements and setting reasonable expectations for the workload. Offer training and support for stress management and resilience. Encourage employees to take breaks and prioritize self-care.

To Empower your colleagues is to 'Give Power'.

Empowering means **giving them the freedom and support to make decisions, take risks, and develop their skills and expertise**. Here are some ways to empower members of your team:

Provide clear direction and communicate expectations to your team. This clarity helps ensure everyone is aligned with the team's and organisation's goals and objectives.

Delegate responsibility and allow team members to make decisions and take ownership of their work. This freedom helps to build trust and confidence and allows team members to develop their skills and expertise.

Encourage creativity and innovation by providing opportunities for team members to share their ideas and perspectives. These opportunities can lead to new approaches and solutions that benefit the team and the organisation.

Provide support and resources to help team members be successful in their roles. This support can include training, coaching, and access to tools and technologies to enhance their work.

Foster a culture of trust and respect by encouraging open communication, collaboration, and teamwork. This helps to create a positive and supportive work environment where team members feel valued and empowered.

Recognise and reward employees for their contributions to the change process. This recognition can be through verbal recognition, promotions, or bonuses. This acknowledgement helps reinforce the importance of the change and the contributions of individual employees, reinforces the importance of high performance, and creates a culture of excellence.

Summarising practices to implement to empower project managers and teams

Provide clear direction: Provide clear direction and communicate expectations to your team.

Delegate responsibility: Delegate responsibility and give team members the freedom to make decisions and take ownership of their work.

Encourage creativity and innovation: Encourage creativity and innovation by providing opportunities for team members to share their ideas and perspectives.

Provide support and resources: Provide support and resources to help team members be successful in their roles.

Foster a culture of trust and respect: Foster a culture of trust and respect by encouraging open communication, collaboration, and teamwork.

Recognise and reward employees: Recognise and reward employees for their contributions to the change process.

By implementing these strategies, you can empower your team members and create a culture of excellence and innovation that benefits the team and the organisation.

Effective types of reward and recognition

Here is a summary list of popular methods of recognising and motivating staff for performance above and beyond the Call of Duty. We say above and beyond because corporations, such as IBM and Microsoft, do not believe in celebrating or rewarding average performance or meeting the base requirements of your job. After all, that is what you are paid to do anyway.

Verbal recognition: A supervisor or colleague's sincere appreciation can be a powerful motivator for employees.

Written recognition: A thank-you note, email, or other written message can provide employees with tangible evidence of their accomplishments and reinforce their value to the organization.

Public recognition: Acknowledging an employee's achievements in front of their peers or company-wide meetings can boost morale and create a sense of pride and accomplishment.

Performance-based rewards: Rewards based on specific performance metrics, such as sales quotas or customer satisfaction ratings, can motivate employees to achieve their goals and contribute to the organization's success.

Bonuses: Financial incentives such as bonuses or profit-sharing can provide employees with tangible rewards for their hard work and incentivize continued high performance.

Time off: Providing employees with additional time off, such as a half-day or extra vacation time, can be a valuable reward that helps employees achieve a better work-life balance.

Professional development opportunities: Offering employees opportunities for career advancement, such as training or mentoring programs, can show employees that the organization is invested in their growth and development.

Social recognition: Celebrating employee accomplishments through social media or other public channels can help build a sense of community and pride within the organization.

Employee perks: Offering employees perks such as free food or drinks, gym memberships, or other workplace amenities can create a positive work environment and enhance employee satisfaction.

Customized rewards: Customizing rewards to fit employees' preferences and needs can demonstrate the organization's commitment to employee well-being and create a more personalized and meaningful recognition experience.

Effective reward and recognition programs should be tailored to the organisation's and its employees' specific needs and goals. Regular communication, feedback, and evaluation can help ensure these programs remain effective and relevant.

Evaluate

Evaluating change management involves assessing the effectiveness of the strategies, tools, and techniques to implement a change initiative. Here are some steps you can take to evaluate change management:

Define evaluation criteria: The first step in evaluating change management is to define the evaluation criteria. This definition involves identifying the goals and objectives of the change initiative and the key performance indicators (KPIs) that will be used to measure success.

Collect data: Collect data on the change initiative, including the processes, tools, and techniques used to implement the change. This data collection can include surveys, interviews, focus groups, and other methods.

Analyse the data: Analyse the data to determine the effectiveness of the change initiative. This analysis may involve comparing the data to the evaluation criteria to identify gaps or areas for improvement.

Identify successes and challenges: Identify the successes and challenges of the change initiative, including the factors that contributed to the success and the barriers that prevented success.

Develop an action plan: Based on the data analysis, develop an action plan for improving the change initiative. This plan may involve adjusting the strategies, tools, and techniques to implement the change or developing new approaches to overcome challenges.

Monitor progress: Monitor the progress of the action plan to ensure that the changes are effective in improving the change initiative. This monitoring may involve conducting follow-up surveys or other data collection methods to assess the impact of the changes.

Make ongoing improvements: Improve the change initiative based on the evaluation data and ongoing monitoring. This continual improvement will help ensure that the change initiative continues to meet the goals and objectives of the organisation.

By following these steps, you can effectively evaluate progress in your changes and make ongoing improvements to ensure the initiative's success through the E4XLM change cycle.

Constructive engagement behaviours:

Be open and approachable

Provide a safe environment

Ask for feedback regularly

Provide feedback training

Lead by example

Focus on behaviour, not personality

Follow up on feedback

Encouraging constructive feedback

Encouraging constructive feedback is essential to creating a culture of continuous improvement and growth. Here are some strategies you can use to encourage constructive feedback from your team:

Be open and approachable: Encourage your team members to approach you with their feedback. Make it clear that you are open to hearing their thoughts and ideas.

Provide a safe environment: Create a safe environment where team members feel comfortable expressing their opinions. This environment can be achieved by establishing ground rules for respectful communication and providing constructive and non-threatening feedback.

Ask for feedback regularly: Ask your team members for feedback regularly. This feedback can be done through surveys, one-on-one meetings, or other channels.

Provide feedback training: Provide your team with training on how to give and receive feedback effectively. This enablement can increase the team's confidence in providing constructive feedback.

Lead by example: Lead by example and demonstrate that you are open to receiving feedback. Be open and receptive to feedback, and take action to demonstrate its value.

Focus on behaviour, not personality: Encourage your team to focus on the behaviour and actions they want to change rather than criticising the person. This adjustment can help ensure that feedback is constructive and not personal.

Follow up on feedback: Follow up on feedback by implementing changes and improvements where appropriate.

This follow-up will demonstrate that you value and take your team's feedback seriously.

Using these strategies, you can encourage constructive feedback from your team and create a continuous improvement and growth culture. This culture can help your team to work more effectively together and achieve better outcomes for the project.

Transformational Leadership

The E4 Xchange Leadership Model is a transformational leadership style. Transformational leadership is a leadership style in which a leader inspires and motivates their team to achieve higher performance levels and reach their full potential.

Here are some of the attributes and skills that a transformational leader typically possesses:

Visionary: A transformational leader has a clear and compelling vision for the future that they can communicate to their team in an inspiring way.

Charismatic: Transformational leaders naturally connect with people and inspire them to follow their lead. As a result, they are often seen as charismatic and engaging.

Passionate: Transformational leaders are deeply committed to their vision and are passionate about making it a reality. As a result, they can inspire others with their enthusiasm and energy.

Empathetic: Transformational leaders can put themselves in their team members' shoes and understand their perspectives and concerns. They are supportive and encouraging and listen actively to feedback and ideas.

Inspirational: Transformational leaders can inspire their teams to achieve great things by setting high standards and leading by example. As a result, they are optimistic and optimistic, and they inspire confidence in their team members.

Innovative: Transformational leaders are creative and innovative, always looking for new ways to improve processes and achieve better outcomes. They encourage team members to think outside the box and take calculated risks.

Collaborative: Transformational leaders can build strong relationships with their team members and foster collaboration and teamwork. They are inclusive and supportive, and they value diverse perspectives and ideas.

Coach: Transformational leaders act as coaches and mentors, providing guidance and support to help their team members grow and develop. They are invested in their team members' success and are committed to helping them achieve their goals.

Transformational leaders inspire and motivate their teams to achieve greatness by setting a clear vision, communicating effectively, and leading by example. They are passionate, innovative, empathetic, and collaborative and invest in their team members' growth and development.

***

In the book's final section, we will build your Playbook for creating a resilient project management and delivery culture.

Part 4
Building your project management and service delivery playbook for a resilient delivery culture

Building your playbook

This point in the book is where the rubber hits the road as we build out your unique project delivery culture playbook considering everything we have learned up until now. It is not reasonable to replicate all of the good practices in the book's first part without applying your mind to your own organisational culture and climate and defining what you want to do more of, less of, and differently, to build a resilient delivery environment and culture.

What should be in a project delivery vision statement?

A project delivery vision statement is a high-level statement that describes a project's desired outcome and purpose. It should be concise, inspiring, and provide a clear direction for the project team.

A project delivery vision statement includes:

Project Goal

Benefit to Stakeholders

Target Market

Unique Value Proposition

Timeline

Team Values

A project delivery vision statement

Some key components that should be included in a project delivery vision statement may include:

Project Goal: The vision statement should describe the ultimate goal or objective of the project. It should be specific, measurable, and aligned with the organisation's strategic objectives.

Benefit to Stakeholders: The vision statement should clearly articulate the benefits that the project will deliver to the stakeholders, whether they are customers, partners, employees, or the organisation as a whole. This clarity can help build buy-in and support for the project.

Target Market: If the project is focused on a specific market or target audience, the vision statement should identify who the project is for and how it will meet their needs.

Unique Value Proposition: The vision statement should describe the unique value proposition that the project will provide to the stakeholders. This value proposition can help differentiate the project from other initiatives and reinforce the importance of the project.

Timeline: The vision statement should include a general timeline or timeframe for the project. This timeline can help align expectations and build urgency for the project team.

Team Values: If a team executes the project, the vision statement should describe the team's values, culture, and approach to delivering the project. This statement can help build team cohesion and provide a shared sense of purpose.

Overall, a project delivery vision statement should be an aspirational statement that inspires and motivates the project team and stakeholders to work towards a common goal. It should be communicated clearly and consistently throughout the project to ensure alignment and a shared understanding of its purpose and goals.

*A project **team** mission statement may include:*

Project Goals

Team Values

Team Roles and Responsibilities

Project Scope

Stakeholder Engagement

Continuous Improvement

What should be in a project team mission statement?

A project team mission statement is a high-level statement that outlines a project team's purpose, values, and goals. It should provide a clear and concise direction for the team, align with the overall project objectives, and serve as a guiding principle for team decision-making. Some key components that should be included in a project team mission statement may include:

Project Goals: The mission statement should articulate the specific goals and objectives of the project team. It should be clear, measurable, and aligned with the project objectives.

Team Values: The mission statement should outline the values and principles that guide the behaviour and decisions of the team. These values and principles may include collaboration, communication, accountability, integrity, and a focus on delivering high-quality results.

Team Roles and Responsibilities: The mission statement should define the roles and responsibilities of each team member and how they contribute to the project's success. It should clarify team members' expectations and ensure everyone is aligned and focused on the same goals.

Project Scope: The mission statement should outline the project's scope, including the deliverables, timeline, and budget. It should clarify the project parameters and ensure the team is aligned with the project scope.

Stakeholder Engagement: The mission statement should emphasise the importance of stakeholder engagement, including communication and collaboration with key stakeholders such as customers, sponsors, and partners. It should ensure that the team is focused on delivering value to the stakeholders and meeting their needs.

Continuous Improvement: The mission statement should promote a culture of continuous improvement, including learning from past experiences and incorporating feedback into the project. It should encourage the team to strive for excellence and continuously improve their processes and results.

Overall, a project team mission statement should be an aspirational statement that inspires and motivates the team to work towards a common goal. It should be communicated clearly and consistently to the team to ensure alignment and a shared understanding of the project's purpose and goals.

***

Now we get down to the brass tacks of building a playbook for creating or recovering your organisation's resilient project management delivery culture.

As mentioned at the beginning of the book, you will most likely benefit from engaging specialists from your internal organisational development area or external consultants specialising in organisational development and change. As good as the book and our course are, there is no substitute for setting goals specific to your organisational context and having an outside party give you their perspective as you progress along the spectrum.

At the beginning of each section or under each major heading, you will see an example of how you might describe an ambition for that particular element of building a resilient delivery culture. As mentioned above, you need to ensure that this statement is aligned with your organisation's strategic and tactical goals and not created in a vacuum. You will only get the buy-in and commitment of resources if the organisation sees that alignment.

Examples of project delivery vision statements:

A software development department:

Our department's project delivery vision statement is to deliver high-quality software solutions that exceed client expectations consistently. We strive to foster a collaborative and innovative environment where our team members are empowered to explore new technologies, methodologies, and approaches. Through effective communication, efficient project management, and continuous improvement, we aim to deliver projects on time, within budget, and with the utmost attention to detail. Our ultimate goal is to establish our department as a trusted partner known for delivering exceptional software products that drive client success.

A hospital project delivery team:

Our project delivery vision statement for our hospital group is to provide exceptional healthcare services through efficient and effective project management. We are committed to delivering projects that improve patient care, enhance operational efficiency, and drive positive outcomes for our community. By fostering a culture of collaboration, innovation, and continuous improvement, we aim to deliver projects on time, within budget, and in alignment with the highest quality and safety standards. Our vision is to be recognised as a leading healthcare organisation that consistently delivers successful projects, enabling us to provide exceptional care and improve our patients' overall health and well-being.

A civil engineering company

Our project delivery vision statement for our civil engineering project management function is to lead the successful execution of construction projects, delivering infrastructure solutions that positively impact communities. We strive to be at the forefront of innovative project management practices, leveraging cutting-edge technology and methodologies to optimise project outcomes. Through effective planning, coordination, and stakeholder engagement, we aim to deliver projects on time, within budget, and to the highest quality and sustainability standards. Our vision is to be recognised as a trusted and reliable partner known for delivering complex civil engineering projects that enhance infrastructure, promote economic growth, and improve the overall quality of life for people in the communities we serve

Your Vision:
We envision a resilient project delivery culture and a favourable climate that motivates, attracts and retains talented project managers.

Options we have available to us are:

The next steps are:

Who

Will do what

By when

Guiding Principles for your project delivery culture while building this Playbook:

Here is a set of guiding principles for all project and service delivery staff. Examples of guiding principles are:

- In today's constantly evolving world, possessing the skill of adaptive leadership is highly advantageous. Leaders who navigate new challenges and situations effectively can successfully steer their teams towards achieving their goals. To do so, they must possess a deep understanding of themselves and possess the capability to make swift decisions based on newly acquired information. By embracing the concept of adaptive leadership, we can pave the way for a brighter future for ourselves and the people around us.
- To achieve success, it is essential to align our objectives and strategy. Therefore, we should focus on creating value that aligns with our goals and purpose.
- Establishing effective governance is a key factor in the success of any organisation. It necessitates dedication to equity, openness, and responsibility. By giving importance to these principles, we can foster a climate of confidence and admiration that encourages everyone to perform optimally. So let's welcome the concepts of proper governance and collaborate to build a better future for everyone.
- Maintaining a strong emphasis on the benefits for the business is crucial.
- Establishing clear roles and responsibilities empowers individuals to take ownership and accountability for their actions, leading to a greater sense of purpose and productivity.

- Success can only be achieved through collaboration. This is why it's crucial to encourage a culture of teamwork among departments, teams, and individuals. Together, we can reach new heights and accomplish amazing things. Communication should be continuous and clear,
- Adopting a consultative approach can bring about positive change and growth. We can achieve greater success and make more informed decisions by seeking input and collaborating with others. So let us embrace this approach and work together towards a brighter future.
- Mastering the art of managing projects with precision and skill is a testament to one's ability to lead and succeed. Showcasing your control and expertise in this area will inspire those around you and pave the way for continued growth and achievement. Learning from experience,
- Managing by stages is a powerful way to manage and achieve success. This approach allows for a clear and organised path towards achieving goals. It enables leaders to focus on each stage and ensure that every step towards success is taken carefully and thoughtfully. By managing by stages, leaders can ensure that their team is on track and that progress is being made towards the ultimate goal. This approach promotes accountability, efficiency, and success. With a strong focus on each stage, leaders can inspire their team to achieve great things and create a culture of excellence.
- Embracing systems thinking can lead to a deeper understanding of the interconnectedness of our world and how our actions can have a ripple effect on everything around us. Considering the whole system

and its parts, we can identify opportunities for positive change and create solutions that benefit everyone involved.
- Adapting the project management system to be appropriate can unquestionably boost efficiency and magnify success.

High-performing teams

Examples of 'what good looks like for a project team

1. High Performing Team in Engineering:

An engineering team that consistently delivers exceptional results meets project milestones, and exceeds client expectations can be considered a high-performing team. They demonstrate strong technical expertise, effective collaboration, and innovative problem-solving skills. This team maintains high productivity, efficiency, and quality throughout the project lifecycle while fostering a positive and supportive team culture.

2. High Performing Team in Software Engineering:

A high-performing software engineering team is characterised by their ability to deliver high-quality software solutions on time and within budget consistently. They exhibit strong technical skills, expertise in various programming languages and frameworks, and a deep understanding of software development best practices. This team embraces Agile methodologies, such as Scrum or Kanban, enabling efficient collaboration, continuous improvement, and rapid adaptation to changing project requirements.

3. High Performing Team in Healthcare:

A high-performing healthcare team provides exceptional patient care, demonstrates excellent clinical outcomes, and operates efficiently. They exhibit strong medical knowledge, effective interdisciplinary collaboration, and a patient-centred approach. This team excels in communication, both within the team and with patients and their families, ensuring a seamless and coordinated care experience. They prioritise patient safety, follow evidence-based practices, and continuously seek ways to enhance the quality and efficiency of healthcare delivery.

What good looks like for our teams, and what we will do to achieve and sustain it

(Eg. We will determine a set of standards which are universally accepted within the organisation as being characteristic of a healthy project delivery environment in terms of how we do things and how we feel about how we do things.)

Options we have available to us are:

Next steps are:

Who

Will do what

By when

Poor project delivery

1. Poor Project Delivery in Engineering:

Poor project delivery in engineering may involve frequent delays, cost overruns, and compromised quality. The project may suffer from inadequate planning, unrealistic timelines, and poor risk management. Inadequate coordination among engineering disciplines, miscommunication, and lack of stakeholder engagement can contribute to poor project outcomes. Failure to adhere to industry standards and regulations may also lead to safety issues and legal consequences.

2. Poor Project Delivery in Software Engineering:

In software engineering, poor project delivery may involve significant bugs or defects in the software, missed deadlines, and incomplete features. This can result from poor requirements gathering and documentation, inadequate testing and quality assurance processes, and insufficient collaboration between developers and stakeholders. Poor project management practices, such as scope creep, inadequate resource allocation, and lack of clear communication, can also contribute to subpar project outcomes.

3. Poor Project Delivery in Healthcare:

Poor project delivery in healthcare can manifest as the delayed implementation of new systems or processes, cost overruns, and failure to achieve intended benefits. This may occur due to inadequate stakeholder engagement and buy-in, insufficient training and support for staff, and resistance to change. Inadequate planning and coordination, coupled with limited consideration of the impact on patient care and workflow, can lead to disruptions, inefficiencies, and dissatisfaction among healthcare providers and patients.

What poor delivery looks like for us, and what will we do to improve it

(Eg. We will draw on our lessons learned and industry case studies to determine what poor delivery looks like within our organisation. We will focus on management styles affecting the delivery culture and the climate within the organisation.)

Options we have available to us are:

Next steps are:

Who

Will do what

By when

Key health indicators

1. Key Project Health Indicators in Engineering:

a) Schedule Performance: Assessing the project's adherence to the planned schedule, monitoring milestones, and measuring the percentage of work completed against the planned timeline.

b) Cost Performance: Tracking the project's financial performance by comparing actual and budgeted costs, evaluating cost variances, and identifying cost overruns.

c) Quality Metrics: Monitoring and evaluating the quality of deliverables, adherence to engineering standards, and identifying any defects or rework required.

d) Safety Performance: Assessing and ensuring compliance with safety protocols and regulations, tracking incident rates, and monitoring the implementation of safety measures.

2. Key Project Health Indicators in Software Engineering:

a) Delivery Time: Monitoring the project's progress against the planned timeline, tracking milestones, and assessing any delays or schedule slippage.

b) Defect Density: Measuring the number of defects or bugs discovered per unit of code or software module, evaluating the severity of defects, and ensuring proper bug tracking and resolution processes are in place.

c) Customer Satisfaction: Collect feedback from stakeholders, users, and clients to gauge their satisfaction with the software's functionality, usability, and overall performance.

d) Agile Metrics (if using Agile methodologies): Tracking metrics such as velocity, sprint burndown, and backlog health to evaluate the team's efficiency and predictability.

3. Key Project Health Indicators in Healthcare:

a) Patient Satisfaction: Gathering patient feedback to evaluate their satisfaction with the healthcare services, including factors such as communication, responsiveness, and overall experience.

b) Clinical Outcomes: Monitoring and measuring key health indicators and patient outcomes to assess the effectiveness and impact of the implemented healthcare interventions or projects.

c) Resource Utilisation: Tracking the efficient utilisation of healthcare resources such as beds, equipment, and staff and ensuring optimal allocation to meet patient needs.

d) Adherence to Regulatory Standards: Ensuring compliance with relevant healthcare regulations, protocols, and accreditation standards, such as HIPAA (Health Insurance Portability and Accountability Act) or Joint Commission requirements.

Key health indicators that will guide us

(Eg. We will define our key health indicators and the criteria by which they will be rated red, amber or green. This definition is directly related to the exception approach, which we will define. We intend to create a delivery environment where our definitions are applied consistently by project managers and managers.)

Options we have available to us are:

Next steps are:

Who

Will do what

By when

Managing by Exception

Managing projects by exception involves defining tolerances for key project aspects and empowering project managers to make decisions within those boundaries. Here are examples of managing projects by exception in engineering, software engineering, and healthcare:

1. Engineering:

In an engineering project, the project manager may establish tolerances for the project schedule and cost. For example, the project manager sets a tolerance of ±5% for the project duration and ±10% for the project budget. If the project is progressing within these tolerances, the project manager can continue managing the project without intervention from higher-level management. However, if the project exceeds these tolerances, it triggers an exception and requires the project manager to escalate the situation to higher management levels for review and decision-making.

2. Software Engineering:

In a software engineering project, the project manager may define tolerances for deliverables and quality metrics. For instance, the project manager sets a tolerance of no more than 5% defects per module and requires at least 90% of planned features to be implemented. If the project stays within these tolerances, the project manager can manage the project autonomously. But if the quality metrics or feature implementation deviates beyond these tolerances, an exception is raised, prompting the project manager to escalate the situation for further review and decision-making.

3. Healthcare:

In a healthcare project, the project manager may establish tolerances for patient satisfaction and clinical outcomes. For example, the project manager sets a tolerance of at least an

80% patient satisfaction rate and requires a minimum 10% reduction in readmission rates. If the project achieves or exceeds these tolerances, the project manager continues managing the project without intervention. However, if the tolerances are not met, an exception is declared, and the project manager escalates the situation to higher management levels for assessment and decision-making.

Managing projects by exception empowers project managers to exercise authority and make day-to-day decisions within predetermined tolerances in all three domains. Exceptions trigger a review process to evaluate and determine whether adjustments or interventions are necessary to bring the project back within acceptable limits.

Exception approach

(Eg. We will define our approach to managing by exception. We will make it clear what we consider acceptable tolerances by which project managers can determine when they should bring any deviation to the attention of the project board. These tolerances will be agreed upon on a project-by-project basis, and it will be apparent to the project manager that we do not punish timely reporting of potential issues.)

Options we have available to us are:

Next steps are:

Who

Will do what

By when

Project Management methodologies in industries

1. Engineering:

a) Waterfall: A traditional sequential project management methodology commonly used in engineering projects. It follows a linear progression through different project phases, including requirements gathering, design, implementation, testing, and deployment.

b) Agile: Agile methodologies like Scrum or Kanban are increasingly adopted in engineering projects. They emphasise iterative development, flexibility, and close collaboration between cross-functional teams to deliver value in shorter cycles.

2. Software Engineering:

a) Agile (Scrum): Scrum is a popular Agile framework used in software engineering projects. It involves breaking down the project into time-boxed iterations called sprints, focusing on delivering working software in each sprint through frequent feedback, collaboration, and adaptability.

b) DevOps: DevOps is a project management methodology that emphasises the collaboration and integration of development (Dev) and operations (Ops) teams. It aims to streamline software delivery, automate processes, and ensure continuous integration, deployment, and monitoring.

3. Healthcare:

a) Lean Six Sigma: A project management methodology that combines Lean principles (eliminating waste) with Six Sigma methodologies (reducing variability) to improve processes and reduce defects or errors in healthcare delivery.

b) PRINCE2 (Projects IN Controlled Environments): PRINCE2 is a structured project management methodology widely used in healthcare projects. It provides a framework for managing projects by defining clear roles, stages, and processes, emphasising controlled and effective project delivery.

Project management methodologies can be adapted and tailored to fit the specific needs and characteristics of each industry or project within that industry.

Project Delivery Methodology:

We will outline the organisation's preferred project delivery methodology, including a step-by-step process for executing projects.

Options we have available to us are:

Next steps are:

Who

Will do what

By when

Project Management tools

1. Engineering:

a) Autodesk Construction Cloud: A comprehensive project management platform for the construction industry that includes tools for project planning, collaboration, document management, and field management.

b) Procore: A widely used construction project management software that offers features for project scheduling, document control, budgeting, change management, and communication.

2. Software Engineering:

a) JIRA: A popular issue-tracking and project management software used by development teams. It allows agile project management, issue tracking, release management, and collaboration.

b) Asana: A flexible project management tool that enables software engineering teams to plan, track, and manage tasks, assign work, collaborate, and monitor project progress.

3. Healthcare:

a) Epic Systems: An electronic health record (EHR) system widely used in healthcare organisations. It includes project management functionalities for healthcare projects, such as task tracking, collaboration, and integration with clinical workflows.

b) CareCloud: A healthcare practice management software that includes project management features to facilitate scheduling, task assignment, and collaboration among healthcare professionals.

These examples provide a glimpse of project management software commonly used in each industry. However, numerous other options are available, and the selection depends on the specific needs and requirements of the project and organisation.

Project Management Tools:
We will list the project management tools and software used to manage the project.

Options we have available to us are:

Next steps are:

Who

Will do what

By when

Project Management Roles and Responsibilities

1. Project Board:

The Project Board is responsible for providing strategic oversight, decision-making, and governance for the project. The composition and specific roles within the Project Board may vary but typically include the following:

- Executive Sponsor: Provides overall project vision, secures necessary resources, and champions the project at a senior management level.
- Project Sponsor: Acts as a key advocate for the project, supports the Project Manager, and ensures alignment with organisational goals.
- Senior Stakeholders: Represents various stakeholders and provide input, feedback, and approvals throughout the project lifecycle.
- Subject Matter Experts: Contribute specialised knowledge and expertise in the project domain, offering guidance and support.

The Project Board's key responsibilities include:

- Setting project objectives, scope, and overall direction.
- Approving project plans, budgets, and major decisions.
- Monitoring project progress, risks, and issues.
- Providing guidance and support to the Project Manager.
- Making critical decisions and resolving escalated issues.

2. Project Manager:

The Project Manager is responsible for the day-to-day management and successful project delivery. Their role encompasses various aspects of project planning, execution, and control. Key responsibilities include:

- Project Planning: Developing project plans and defining objectives, scope, timelines, and resource requirements.
- Team Leadership: Building and leading the project team, assigning tasks, and fostering collaboration.
- Stakeholder Management: Identifying stakeholders, managing expectations, and ensuring effective communication.
- Risk Management: Identifying and assessing risks, developing mitigation strategies, and monitoring risk throughout the project.
- Monitoring and Control: Tracking project progress, managing resources, controlling budget, and ensuring adherence to timelines.
- Issue Resolution: Identifying and resolving project issues, conflicts, and obstacles that may impact project success.
- Reporting: Providing regular project status updates and progress reports and presenting project performance to the Project Board.

3. Team Manager:

In some projects, a Team Manager role may exist to oversee the day-to-day activities and performance of a specific team within the project. This role is responsible for the following:

- Managing the team's workload, assignments, and performance.

- Providing guidance, mentorship, and support to team members.
- Ensuring effective coordination and collaboration within the team.
- Monitoring team progress and addressing any issues or conflicts.
- Facilitating communication between the team and the Project Manager.
- Contributing to overall project planning, decision-making, and problem-solving.

The specific roles and responsibilities of a Team Manager may vary depending on the project's context, size, and organisational structure.

Roles and Responsibilities:

We will describe the roles and responsibilities of project team members, stakeholders, and other contributors involved in project delivery.

Options we have available to us are:

Next steps are:

Who

Will do what

By when

Project Team Management Principles

Project team management principles guide resilient project teams' effective management and leadership.

To ensure project success, it's crucial to establish open communication channels that promote transparency and understanding. Collaboration and teamwork are equally important in leveraging diverse expertise and encouraging cross-functional cooperation. Effective leadership plays a significant role in empowering team members to make decisions within their areas of responsibility, leading to innovation and autonomy.

Encouraging continuous learning and improvement fosters a culture of feedback and professional development opportunities. In addition, adaptability and flexibility help respond effectively to project scope or requirements changes. Lastly, upholding ethical standards and professionalism in all project activities maintains integrity, honesty, and accountability among team members and stakeholders.

These principles guide effective project team management in engineering, software engineering, and healthcare projects. Tailor and adapt these principles to suit each project's requirements and context.

Team management

(Eg. We will implement a leadership development plan that spans all levels of leadership and management within the organisation. We aim to develop a culture of leadership that embraces diversity and recognises the unique gifts of employees so they can make the most of their strengths in delivering project outcomes.

We will create an environment where project managers feel supported in managing their teams and having forthright conversations with stakeholders horizontally and vertically up into the parent organisation.)

Options we have available to us are:

Next steps are:

Who

Will do what

By when

Risk Management examples

1. Engineering Projects:

a) Risk: Unforeseen ground conditions during construction.

Mitigation: Conduct thorough geotechnical surveys and soil testing before construction to identify potential ground conditions. Develop contingency plans and allocate appropriate resources for potential ground condition variations.

b) Risk: Supply chain disruptions impacting material availability.

Mitigation: Maintain multiple suppliers and establish backup plans. Regularly monitor supplier performance and establish alternative sourcing options. Maintain a buffer stock of critical materials.

c) Risk: Weather-related delays affecting project timelines.

Mitigation: Monitor weather forecasts and develop contingency plans for adverse weather conditions. Incorporate weather-related buffers into project schedules. Implement strategies such as temporary shelters or alternative work areas to minimise weather impacts.

2. Software Engineering Projects:

a) Risk: Unclear or changing project requirements.

Mitigation: Conduct thorough requirement gathering and analysis at the project's outset. Establish a change management process to handle requirement changes. Maintain regular communication and collaboration with stakeholders to ensure clarity and alignment.

b) Risk: Technical dependencies and integration challenges.

Mitigation: Conduct a comprehensive assessment of technical dependencies early in the project. Develop a clear integration strategy and establish regular communication channels between teams. Conduct integration testing and resolve issues proactively.

c) Risk: Data security and privacy breaches.

Mitigation: Implement robust security measures, such as encryption, access controls, and regular security assessments. Adhere to industry best practices and compliance regulations. Conduct regular security audits and training for team members.

3. Healthcare Projects:
a) Risk: Changes in regulatory requirements impacting project compliance.

Mitigation: Stay updated on regulatory changes and ensure project plans and processes align with the latest requirements. Engage regulatory experts to provide guidance. Conduct regular audits and assessments to ensure ongoing compliance.

b) Risk: Inadequate stakeholder engagement and resistance to change.

Mitigation: Develop a comprehensive stakeholder engagement plan. Communicate project objectives, benefits, and expected outcomes clearly to stakeholders. Involve stakeholders in decision-making and address their concerns through effective communication and change management strategies.

c) Risk: Patient safety incidents or adverse events.

Mitigation: Implement rigorous quality assurance and risk management protocols. Conduct regular safety assessments and implement preventive measures. Ensure comprehensive training for healthcare professionals on safety protocols and incident reporting.

These examples illustrate common risk scenarios and their corresponding mitigation strategies in engineering, software engineering, and healthcare projects. However, risk management should be tailored to each project, considering its unique characteristics, context, and stakeholder requirements.

Risk Management:
We will identify potential risks and describe the organisation's approach to managing and mitigating them.

Options we have available to us are:

Next steps are:

Who

Will do what

By when

Change Management failures

Examples of poor change control in engineering, software engineering, and healthcare projects can lead to negative consequences and project inefficiencies. Here are some examples:

1. Engineering Projects:

a) Unauthorised Scope Creep: Changes to the project scope are implemented without proper evaluation or approval, leading to an uncontrolled expansion of project deliverables. This can result in schedule delays, budget overruns, and compromised project quality.

b) Inadequate Impact Assessment: Changes are implemented without a thorough assessment of their potential impact on project objectives, resources, and constraints. This can lead to unforeseen complications, conflicts, and disruptions in project execution.

c) Lack of Documentation and Tracking: Changes are not adequately documented or tracked, making it difficult to trace their origin, assess their impact, or communicate them effectively to project stakeholders. This can lead to confusion, miscommunication, and difficulty managing project changes.

2. Software Engineering Projects:

a) Frequent Scope Changes: Frequent and uncontrolled changes to software requirements without proper evaluation or prioritisation can result in scope volatility, resource allocation issues, and increased development time.

b) Insufficient Change Impact Assessment: Changes are implemented without a comprehensive assessment of their impact on the software architecture, development effort, or project timeline. This can lead to technical debt, increased risk of defects, and compromised system performance.

c) Lack of Change Control Documentation: Changes are not adequately documented, including change requests, approvals, and related discussions. This lack of documentation hampers proper change tracking, evaluation, and communication, leading to confusion and inefficiencies.

3. Healthcare Projects:

a) Failure to Assess Regulatory Compliance: Changes in healthcare projects that impact regulatory compliance are not adequately assessed or addressed. This can result in non-compliance issues, regulatory penalties, and compromised patient safety.

b) Ineffective Stakeholder Engagement: Changes are implemented without proper engagement and consultation with relevant stakeholders, such as healthcare professionals, administrators, or patients. This lack of involvement can lead to resistance, low adoption rates, and compromised project success.

c) Inadequate Change Communication: Changes are not effectively communicated to all stakeholders, leading to misunderstandings, resistance, and a lack of buy-in. This can result in project delays, increased costs, and reduced overall project effectiveness.

These examples highlight the negative impacts of poor change control practices in engineering, software engineering, and healthcare projects. Conversely, implementing robust change control processes and adhering to best practices can help mitigate risks and ensure successful project outcomes.

Change Management:

We will outline how project scope, timeline, or budget changes will be managed and communicated.

Options we have available to us are:

Next steps are:

Who

Will do what

By when

Project Quality Assurance

Quality assurance practices are essential in engineering, software engineering, and healthcare projects to ensure deliverables meet the required standards and expectations. Here are examples of quality assurance practices in each domain:

1. Engineering Projects:

a) Inspection and Testing: Conduct thorough inspections and tests at various stages of the project, such as during construction, fabrication, or assembly. This includes checking for compliance with specifications, performing quality control checks, and verifying the functionality and safety of components or systems.

b) Quality Audits: Performing regular internal and external audits to assess project processes, adherence to quality standards, and compliance with regulations. These audits help identify areas for improvement, ensure consistency, and maintain quality control throughout the project lifecycle.

c) Documentation and Documentation Control: Implementing robust document control processes to manage project documentation, including design drawings, specifications, test reports, and change control records. This ensures that the latest and approved documentation is accessible, accurate, and maintained in a controlled manner.

2. Software Engineering Projects:

a) Code Reviews: Conducting systematic code reviews to evaluate software code quality, readability, and maintainability. Code reviews help identify and address coding errors, performance bottlenecks, and adherence to coding standards or best practices.

b) Automated Testing: Utilising automated testing frameworks and tools to perform unit tests, integration tests, and system tests. Automated testing helps ensure software functions as intended, detects bugs or defects early and enables efficient regression testing.

c) User Acceptance Testing (UAT): Involving end users or stakeholders in the UAT process to validate that the software meets their requirements and expectations. UAT tests software from a user's perspective, ensuring usability, functionality, and user experience align with desired outcomes.

3. Healthcare Projects:

a) Clinical Protocols and Guidelines: Implementing evidence-based clinical protocols and guidelines to standardise healthcare practices and ensure consistency in delivering quality care. These protocols and guidelines help minimise errors, improve patient outcomes, and promote best practices.

b) Peer Review: Engaging healthcare professionals to perform peer reviews of medical records, diagnoses, treatment plans, or surgical procedures. Peer review helps identify opportunities for improvement, ensure compliance with standards, and enhance patient safety.

c) Patient Satisfaction Surveys: Collecting patient feedback to assess their satisfaction with healthcare services. Patient satisfaction surveys provide insights into areas for improvement, identify gaps in service delivery, and help enhance the overall patient experience.

These examples illustrate common quality assurance practices in engineering, software engineering, and healthcare projects. Adapting and tailoring these practices to each project and industry's specific requirements, standards, and regulations is important.

Quality Assurance:

We will have quality assurance procedures and standards that will be followed to ensure project deliverables meet the required standards.

Options we have available to us are:

Next steps are:

Who

Will do what

By when

Project Delivery Assurance

To audit whether a project delivery plan is being followed, you can follow these steps:

1. Review the Project Delivery Plan: Start by thoroughly reviewing the project delivery plan to understand the intended approach, milestones, deliverables, and timelines. Familiarise yourself with the documented objectives, scope, and key performance indicators.

2. Collect Project Documentation: Gather relevant project documentation, including project schedules, progress reports, meeting minutes, change control records, and other artefacts that provide insights into the project's execution.

3. Compare Actual Progress to Planned Milestones: Assess the project's current status by comparing the actual progress against the planned milestones and deliverables outlined in the project delivery plan. Look for any discrepancies or delays and evaluate the impact on the overall project timeline.

4. Analyse Resource Allocation: Review resource allocation, including human resources, equipment, and budget, to ensure they align with the project plan. Verify that the assigned resources are being utilised effectively and that any deviations from the plan are adequately justified.

5. Evaluate Stakeholder Engagement: Assess stakeholder engagement and communication level by reviewing meeting minutes, correspondence, and stakeholder feedback. Look for evidence of regular and effective communication with project stakeholders to ensure their involvement and alignment with project goals.

6. Assess Risk and Issue Management: Evaluate how risks and issues are managed throughout the project. For example, review risk registers, issue logs, and mitigation plans to determine if identified risks and issues are being actively monitored and addressed according to the project delivery plan.

7. Verify Change Control Process: Examine the change control process to ensure that changes to the project scope, requirements, or timeline are being appropriately evaluated, approved, and documented. In addition, check if changes are incorporated into the project plan and communicated to stakeholders.

8. Conduct Interviews and Discussions: Engage with project team members and key stakeholders through interviews or discussions to gather their perspectives on project execution. Seek feedback on adherence to the project delivery plan, potential challenges, and areas of improvement.

9. Document Findings and Recommendations: Document your findings from the audit, including any deviations or non-compliance with the project delivery plan. Identify areas of concern or improvement and provide recommendations to address the gaps or issues.

10. Communicate Audit Results: Present the audit findings, recommendations, and suggested corrective actions to project stakeholders, including the project manager and project board. Ensure the audit report is clear, concise, and actionable, facilitating discussions and decision-making.

By following these steps, you can conduct a project audit to assess whether the project delivery plan is being followed. The audit helps identify deviations, risks, or areas for improvement, enabling timely corrective actions and ensuring project success.

Project Assurance:
We will include project assurance procedures and standards that will be followed to ensure project deliverables meet the required standards.

Options we have available to us are:

Next steps are:

Who

Will do what

By when

Stakeholder Communication

Effective stakeholder communication is crucial for successful project management in engineering, software engineering, and healthcare projects. Here are examples of stakeholder communication practices in each domain:

1. Engineering Projects:

a) Regular Progress Updates: Providing periodic progress updates to stakeholders, including clients, project sponsors, and regulatory authorities. This can be done through progress reports, status meetings, or site visits, ensuring stakeholders are informed about project milestones, challenges, and achievements.

b) Change Management Communication: Effectively communicate any project scope, design, or specifications changes to stakeholders. This involves clarifying the proposed changes and their impact on project objectives and timelines and soliciting feedback or approvals as necessary.

c) Stakeholder Engagement Meetings: Conduct stakeholder engagement meetings to foster collaboration, gather input, and address concerns. These meetings provide a platform for stakeholders to share their perspectives, provide feedback, and stay actively engaged in the project.

2. Software Engineering Projects:

a) Agile Communication Framework: Adopting agile communication practices, such as daily stand-up meetings, sprint reviews, and retrospectives. These practices facilitate regular communication among team members, product owners, and other stakeholders, enabling transparency, feedback sharing, and alignment.

b) User Story Workshops: Organising user story workshops or requirements gathering sessions with stakeholders to understand their needs, gather requirements, and validate proposed solutions. This collaborative approach ensures that stakeholder expectations are effectively captured and translated into software features.

c) Demo Sessions: Conduct demo sessions to showcase completed functionalities or prototypes to stakeholders. These sessions allow stakeholders to interact with the software, provide feedback, and ensure alignment with their expectations.

3. Healthcare Projects:

a) Patient and Family Engagement: Actively involving patients and their families in healthcare projects through open communication channels. This can include providing clear information about treatment plans, involving them in shared decision-making processes, and seeking their feedback on the quality of care.

b) Effective Team Communication: Promoting effective communication within healthcare teams, including physicians, nurses, administrators, and other stakeholders. This involves regular team meetings, huddles, and shared electronic communication platforms to ensure timely and accurate information sharing.

c) Stakeholder Education and Awareness: Conducting education and awareness campaigns to inform stakeholders, including healthcare professionals, about project objectives, benefits, and anticipated outcomes. This helps generate buy-in, address potential resistance, and foster a positive project environment.

These examples demonstrate various stakeholder communication practices in engineering, software engineering, and healthcare projects. Tailoring communication approaches to the specific project and stakeholders involved is important, considering their unique needs, preferences, and communication channels. Effective communication fosters collaboration, minimises misunderstandings, and promotes project success.

Communication Plan:
We will publish a communication plan that outlines how stakeholders will be informed and engaged throughout the project lifecycle.

Options we have available to us are:

Next steps are:

Who

Will do what

By when

Good Project Closeout

A well-executed project closure is essential for successful completion and transition to the next phase or project. Here are examples of good project closure practices in engineering, software engineering, and healthcare projects:

1. Engineering Projects:

a) Documentation and Handover: Ensure all project documentation, including design specifications, technical drawings, and operation manuals, is finalised, organised, and handed over to the relevant stakeholders. This ensures a smooth transition for ongoing maintenance, future modifications, or new projects.

b) Lessons Learned and Post-Project Evaluation: Conduct a comprehensive review of the project's successes, challenges, and lessons learned. Document the findings and share them with the project team and stakeholders. Use this information to improve future project management practices.

c) Stakeholder Satisfaction Assessment: Gather feedback from stakeholders to assess their satisfaction with the project outcomes, delivery process, and overall experience. Use the feedback to identify areas of improvement and address any outstanding concerns.

2. Software Engineering Projects:

a) Software Release and Deployment: Ensure a well-planned and controlled release and deployment process for the software. This includes coordinating with relevant teams, preparing documentation, conducting user training, and ensuring a smooth transition to the operational environment.

b) Post-Implementation Support and Monitoring: Establish mechanisms for post-implementation support and monitoring to address any issues or bugs arising after the project closure.

Provide efficient support channels and assign dedicated resources to handle post-implementation challenges.

c) Knowledge Transfer and Retention: Facilitate knowledge transfer sessions to ensure that critical project knowledge, such as design decisions, coding practices, and system configurations, are documented and shared with the relevant teams. This helps preserve project knowledge and facilitate future maintenance and enhancements.

3. Healthcare Projects:

a) Patient Handover and Continuity of Care: Ensure a seamless handover and continuity of care for patients involved in the project. Communicate necessary information to healthcare providers to ensure a smooth transition and maintain patient safety and well-being.

b) Evaluation and Reporting: Evaluate the project's impact on patient outcomes, operational efficiency, and adherence to quality standards. Prepare a comprehensive project evaluation report highlighting key achievements, challenges, and recommendations for future projects.

c) Stakeholder Communication and Engagement: Engage with key stakeholders, including healthcare professionals, administrators, and patients, to provide a project closure summary and seek their feedback. Maintain open communication channels and address any remaining concerns or questions.

These examples illustrate good project closure practices in engineering, software, and healthcare projects. By following these practices, organisations can ensure a well-organised and successful project closure, facilitating knowledge transfer and stakeholder satisfaction and setting the stage for future endeavours.

Project Closeout:

We will describe the project closeout process, including the final review, sign-off, and handover to stakeholders.

Options we have available to us are:

Next steps are:

Who

Will do what

By when

Lessons Learned

Lessons learned from troubled projects provide valuable insights for future improvement and can help avoid similar issues. Here are examples of project lessons learned in troubled engineering, software engineering, and healthcare projects:

1. Engineering Projects:

a) Inadequate Risk Assessment: Lesson learned: Conduct a comprehensive risk assessment at the beginning of the project and regularly reassess risks throughout the project lifecycle. This helps identify potential issues and implement proactive risk mitigation strategies.

b) Poor Communication and Collaboration: Lesson learned: Establish clear lines of communication and promote collaboration among project team members and stakeholders. Use effective communication tools and techniques to ensure timely information sharing and alignment.

c) Insufficient Contingency Planning: Lesson learned: Develop contingency plans to address potential project setbacks or unforeseen events. Having backup strategies and resources in place can help minimise the impact of disruptions on project timelines and deliverables.

2. Software Engineering Projects:

a) Inadequate Requirements Gathering: Lesson learned: Invest sufficient time and effort in thorough requirements gathering and analysis. Engage with stakeholders to clearly understand their needs and document detailed requirements to avoid misinterpretations and scope creep.

b) Lack of User Involvement: Lesson learned: Involve end-users and stakeholders throughout the software development process to ensure their needs and expectations are considered.

Regular feedback loops and user acceptance testing help validate the software's usability and functionality.

c) Insufficient Testing and Quality Assurance: Lesson learned: Strongly emphasise rigorous testing and quality assurance processes. Implement comprehensive testing strategies, including unit testing, integration testing, and user acceptance testing, to identify and address defects early in the development cycle.

3. Healthcare Projects:

a) Inadequate Stakeholder Engagement: Lesson learned: Actively engage key stakeholders, including healthcare professionals, administrators, and patients, throughout the project. Involve them in decision-making, gather feedback, and address their concerns to ensure project alignment and success.

b) Insufficient Change Management: Lesson learned: Develop a robust change management process to effectively handle changes in healthcare projects. Properly evaluate and communicate changes to minimise disruption, ensure compliance, and maintain patient safety.

c) Poor Resource Planning: Lesson learned: Conduct thorough resource planning to ensure adequate staffing, equipment, and budget allocation for the project. Regularly review resource needs and adjust accordingly to prevent resource constraints and delays.

These examples highlight lessons learned from troubled engineering, software engineering, and healthcare projects. By identifying and applying these lessons, organisations can enhance their project management practices, improve project outcomes, and mitigate risks in future endeavours.

Lessons Learned:

We will detail how project outcomes will be evaluated and how the organisation will learn from past experiences to improve future projects.

Options we have available to us are:

Next steps are:

Who

Will do what

By when

Glossary:
We will include a glossary of key terms and definitions to ensure a common understanding of project management language within the organisation.

Appendices

Key service delivery measures

Key service delivery measures are metrics used to evaluate a service delivery process's quality, efficiency, and effectiveness. These measures help organisations ensure that they are meeting the needs of their customers and can be used to identify areas for improvement and make data-driven decisions to improve the service delivery process.

Some key service delivery measures may include:

Service quality: This measure assesses the quality of the service delivered to customers, including customer satisfaction, service reliability, and service availability.

Service level agreement (SLA) compliance: This measure assesses whether the service delivery process meets the requirements and expectations in the SLA. It includes metrics such as SLA adherence, response, and resolution time.

First-time resolution (FTR) rate: This measure assesses the percentage of customer issues resolved on the first contact. A high FTR rate indicates that the service delivery process is efficient and effective.

Response time: This measure assesses the time it takes for the service delivery process to respond to customer requests or issues. It includes metrics such as average response time, maximum response time, and response time by channel.

Cost per contact: This measure assesses the service's cost per customer contact. It includes metrics such as the cost of labour, technology, and other resources required to deliver the service.

Customer retention: This measure assesses the percentage of customers who continue to use the service over time. A high customer retention rate indicates that the service is meeting the needs and expectations of customers.

By tracking these key service delivery measures, organisations can gain a comprehensive view of the service delivery process, identify areas for improvement, and make data-driven decisions to improve the quality, efficiency, and effectiveness of the service delivery process.

What should be in a service delivery vision statement?

A service delivery vision statement is a high-level statement that describes the desired outcome and purpose of a service delivery initiative. It should be inspiring, concise, and provide a clear direction for the service delivery team. Some key components that should be included in a service delivery vision statement may include:

Service Vision: The vision statement should describe the ultimate goal or objective of the service delivery initiative. It should be specific, measurable, and aligned with the organisation's strategic objectives.

Customer Benefit: The vision statement should clearly articulate the benefits that the service delivery initiative will deliver to the customers. It should describe how the initiative will address customer pain points, improve customer experience, and differentiate the organisation from its competitors.

Service Quality: The vision statement should describe the desired service quality, including reliability, responsiveness, accessibility, and ease of use. It should emphasise the importance of delivering high-quality services to the customers.

Service Culture: The vision statement should describe the desired service culture, including values, principles, and behaviours that support the service delivery initiative. It should promote a customer-centric culture that prioritises customer needs and feedback.

Brand Image: The vision statement should describe how the service delivery initiative will reinforce the organisation's brand image and reputation. It should emphasise the importance of consistency, trust, and integrity in delivering services.

Innovation: The vision statement should describe how the service delivery initiative will drive innovation and create new customer value. It should encourage experimentation, creativity, and continuous improvement.

Overall, a service delivery vision statement should be an aspirational statement that inspires and motivates the service delivery team and stakeholders to work towards a common goal. It should be communicated clearly and consistently throughout the service delivery initiative to ensure alignment and a shared understanding of its purpose and goals.

Sources of research into project failure?

Research sources into project failure include academic studies, industry reports, and case studies. Some of the most well-known and widely cited sources of research on project failure include:

Standish Group CHAOS Report: The Standish Group has been researching project success and failure rates for many years and publishes its findings in the CHAOS Report. The report provides statistics on the success and failure rates of various types of projects and insights into the causes of project failure.

Project Management Institute (PMI) Research: The PMI is a professional association for project managers and conducts a wide range of research on project management best practices, including risk management, stakeholder engagement, and project success factors.

International Journal of Project Management: This academic journal publishes research articles on various aspects of project management, including project success and failure rates, risk management, stakeholder engagement, and project leadership.

Harvard Business Review: This business publication features articles on various management aspects, including project management. Many articles focus on real-world case studies and best practices for managing complex projects.

Gartner Research: Gartner is a research and advisory firm that provides insights and analysis on various industries, including project management. Its research includes reports on emerging trends, technologies, and best practices for project management.

Project Failure Case Studies: Many organisations publish case studies of failed projects, providing insights into the causes and lessons learned. These case studies can provide valuable insights for project managers looking to avoid similar project failures.

Overall, there are many research sources into project failure. Project managers can benefit from studying and learning from these sources to improve their project management practices.

Which industry has the greatest project manager attrition?

Project manager attrition rates can vary by industry. Still, some evidence suggests that the IT industry may have higher project manager turnover rates than other industries. For example, a study by the Project Management Institute (PMI) found that the global IT industry had an average project manager turnover rate of 23 per cent, compared to a rate of 13 per cent for the overall project management profession.

The study also found that project managers in the IT industry were more likely to leave their current jobs in pursuit of higher salaries, better work-life balance, and opportunities for career growth. In addition, project managers in the IT industry reported feeling more pressure and stress than those in other industries.

However, it's important to note that attrition rates can vary widely based on various factors, including the specific organisation, region, and market conditions. For example, while the IT industry may have higher rates of project manager turnover on average, many organisations in other industries also experience significant turnover in project management roles.

What is the research into project failure?

Much research has been conducted on project failure over the years. Some of the key findings and insights from this research include the following:

High Failure Rates: Numerous studies have shown that many projects fail to deliver their intended outcomes. Depending on the study and the criteria used, failure rates have been estimated to range from 30% to as high as 70%.

Causes of Failure: Research has identified a wide range of factors that contribute to project failure. Common causes include poor planning and scope definition, inadequate communication and stakeholder management, inadequate resources or skill sets, and changing requirements or scope creep.

Impact of Failure: Project failure can have significant consequences for organisations, including financial losses, damage to reputation, loss of stakeholder confidence, and missed opportunities.

Importance of Risk Management: Effective risk management is critical in reducing the likelihood of project failure. Research has shown that organisations that take a proactive approach to risk management are more likely to successfully deliver projects on time, within budget, and to the required quality standards.

Role of Leadership: Research has also highlighted the importance of leadership in project success. Effective project managers and leaders can set clear goals and expectations, motivate and engage team members, and manage risks and issues proactively.

Continuous Improvement: Finally, research has shown that a culture of continuous improvement is essential for reducing the likelihood of project failure. Organisations that learn from past failures and seek to improve their processes and practices are more likely to succeed in future projects.

Overall, research into project failure has provided valuable insights into the factors contributing to project success and failure and has helped inform best practices and methodologies in project management.

One of the most well-known and widely cited research sources on project failure is the **Standish Group CHAOS Report**: The Standish Group has been researching project success and failure rates for many years and publishes its findings in the CHAOS Report. The report provides statistics on the success and failure rates of various types of projects and insights into the causes of project failure.

Let us look at some of the findings of the chaos report 2018.

What are the main findings of the Standish Group CHAOS Report?

The Standish Group has published its CHAOS Report since 1994, providing statistics and insights into various projects' success and failure rates. Here are some of the main findings from the report:

Success rates are improving: The most recent CHAOS Report (2018) found that the project success rate has improved over time. For example, the report states that 44% of projects in 2018 were deemed successful (i.e., delivered on time, on budget, and with the required features and functions), compared to 26% in 2011.

Failure rates remain high: Despite the improvements in success rates, the CHAOS Report notes that a significant proportion of projects still fail to deliver their intended outcomes. For example, in 2018, 29% of projects were deemed to have failed (i.e., cancelled before completion or delivered but not used), while 27% were considered to be challenged (i.e., delivered but over budget, late, or without all of the required features).

Scope creep is a significant challenge: The CHAOS Report identifies scope creep (i.e., the tendency for project requirements to expand or change over time) as a significant challenge for project managers. It notes that scope creep is the most significant contributor to project failure.

Agile methodologies are gaining in popularity: The CHAOS Report notes that the use of agile methodologies (such as Scrum or Kanban) is increasing and that projects managed using agile methods tend to have higher success rates than those managed using traditional waterfall methods.

Communication and stakeholder management are critical success factors: The CHAOS Report highlights the importance of effective communication and stakeholder management in project success. Projects with strong communication and stakeholder management practices tend to have higher success rates than those with weaker practices.

The CHAOS Report provides valuable insights into project success and failure rates, highlighting the importance of effective project management practices in delivering successful outcomes.

Key Research into Toxic Cultures

"The Impact of Toxic Leaders on Organizational Effectiveness" by B.J. Tepper and A.J. Duffy (2009): This study found that leaders who engage in abusive or toxic behaviours can have a significant negative impact on their teams and organisations, including reduced performance, increased turnover, and damage to employee well-being.

"Toxic Workplace Cultures in Construction Projects: An Exploratory Study" by M.A. Al-Ghassani and C.R. Haas (2016): This study explored the prevalence and impact of toxic workplace cultures in construction projects, finding that factors such as poor communication, lack of trust, and negative leadership styles can contribute to a toxic work environment.

"The Impact of Toxic Organizational Culture on Project Management" by T. Rad and S. Levin (2017): This study examined the impact of toxic organisational culture on project management practices, finding that factors such as lack of trust, poor communication, and resistance to change can all contribute to a toxic project culture that undermines project success.

"Toxic Workplace Environments and Employee Health Outcomes in the Construction Industry" by S. Zare and T.M. Williams (2020): This study examined the impact of toxic workplace environments on employee health outcomes in the construction industry, finding that exposure to toxic behaviours and environments can contribute to a range of adverse health outcomes, including anxiety, depression, and burnout.

Printed in Great Britain
by Amazon